Habit Stacking

Achieve Health,Wealth,Mental
Toughness,and Productivity through
Habit Changes

By: Daniel Patterson

Introduction

When you wake up in the morning, identify the tasks that are more important than others or those that are urgent at that time and get started with those first. Whether we agree or not, we are all creatures of habit. All our mornings are filled with habits we have maintained over the years, from brushing teeth to drinking coffee. The difficult thing is when we try to add newer and healthier habits inside our lives and work. However, developing healthier routines could be as simple as just stacking the habits.

What you need to do is sit down and think of your goals and targets. Then think of the habits you need to acquire to complete those goals. Most of these habits take less than thirty minutes to two hours of everyday efforts. However, some of them are so small that they could slip through the cracks in the door.

The premise is to take all the things you are supposed to be doing to achieve the set goals daily and group them together. You can add them in your morning routine or the afternoon routine or even build them into other different parts of your day. This removes the cognitive load and the stress when you realize that "OMG, I am required to do all these twenty different tasks!" Just go through this easy checklist. Perform all these habits in a row, and you will really start your day or end it with a series of great achievements. A lot of these methods can be found in *The Checklist Manifesto* by Atul Gawande. The central idea is to run your life via a set of checklists. There is no need to keep thinking about them all the time. Just pull the checklist of habits and complete from one to seven and then the later to move through the rest of your day.

You will reach a certain point in time when you will not need the checklist anymore. It could be used just as a reminder. Although I know a certain routine and have performed it a dozen times and sometimes a hundred times, we may still want to pull up the checklist in case something has slipped our minds. But for most parts, it is internal. After a while, you will feel that you had the stacks forever. One of the examples is exercise. Many people who don't exercise can come up with creative excuses for why they are not exercising. They have excuses such as "Oh it's cloudy today and might rain, so I can't go out today for my run" or "I forgot my shoes" or "I forgot my bikini pants." There are many such excuses available to people. More examples of their excuses are "I just don't have enough time today" or "I could not sleep well last night." These are all excuses.

A good habit stacking will be to schedule your workout after you wake up in the morning. After waking up, decide at exactly what point of time you are going to work out that day. Also, add thirty minutes of buffer time in case needed. Schedule this in your routine like you would for any other appointment. Check the weather for the day. It may sound unnecessary, but suppose you are going to work out at 4:00 p.m. and there are a thunderstorm and rains expected at the time. You may have easily solved this problem by checking the weather and made suitable adjustments in your schedule. Actually, you can create if-then logical statements for this: "If it is raining, then I will go to the gym but will not miss the exercise."

So you are giving yourselves multiple methods of getting in the daily workout in case something doesn't go as planned in a day. Remember to have a bag of food with you to the exercise in case you feel hungry before the workout. Ensure that you are carrying all the gym equipment.

Little things like these appear silly, but if you stack them together in a small, quick ten-minute routine where you will run down and check ("Do I have all the necessary things with me?"), then it is easy to follow through with your commitment to exercise. This is one example related to exercising. You can do similar things like these to, say, book marketing. I wake up and then go through the top 100 bestsellers list from an online shop like, say, Amazon. That's the way for the writers as they like to see what is happening in the marketplace. They may run through the Amazon ads and perform split tests on my Squeeze pages. These things don't take much time but produce a massive impact on their business. Before starting writing, they would make sure that at least twenty to thirty minutes are spent on these things to help move the things forward for the book sales.

Some people love their coffee in the morning, so they place their vitamin pills and water next to the kettle so that they do not miss taking the medicine. This is also a kind of habit stacking. Take an existing habit and start attaching things to it. Taking the coffee is what can be called an *anchor habit*. It is what one considers as a trigger. So the coffee is the trigger. Then you do something like placing medicines near it. Some people will weigh themselves in the mornings and fill up Contigo bottles. You are supposed to drink eight cups of water every day. Some people would prefer filling an enormous bottle and sip it throughout the day. So it is about things like these. You may wish to start the tea kettle for your wife or do the dishes. Review your goals and prioritize them. Then it is *boom, boom, boom!* Within the first hour or so of the morning, you have accomplished two dozen tasks.

It is believed that the cognitive peak is about one or two hours after waking up. That is the time when your ideas start to percolate, especially in case you are in the middle of an assignment. It is almost like you are doing the task in your mind, and it is particularly more useful for monotonous work such as manual labor. It gives your mind an opportunity to think of the things you need to do for the day. There is something of a period between waking up and getting fully engaged in something. This buffer is required especially when you review the tasks and goals for the day and then start to think about what is required to achieve the goals. You get a bit of excitement, and the motivation is carried on for the major tasks.

Here are some habits that will help the audience better for their careers:

1. Focus and Schedule. Always begin your day by focusing and scheduling, and remember to start with the three MITs (most important things). When you wake up, identify the tasks that are urgent or super important at the moment and get going with those first. One of the highly recommended ways is to start working on the long-term and important items that are not specifically urgent. No one is necessarily beating down the door to get you to work on the task, but you are aware that it is significant for the long-term success. One of the first of the MITs should be this activity.

2. Track Your Time. The second one, although it is a bit of anal-retentive, is to track your time. It works wonders for most people. Actually, create ten to fifteen categories for whatever you are doing for pursuing your career. One of these activities could be e-mailing. Another one could be deep work activity, and another one could be meetings. You should actually break down the things into different sections or buckets and actually track them. There is an app called Timelogger, and it can be found on the internet. You can create various categories on the app itself, and you can also run a timer each time you are performing those activities.

Although it seems a bit obsessive, after completing every month, just look at the different buckets and check out the time spent on those various activities. Analyze your performance for the month. In case you find that you are spending 20 to 30 percent of your time on admin activities that are not helping your career, then maybe you need to start switching things around or try to find other methods to reduce or eliminate the time spent on that specifically wrong category.

3. Use Metrics. You can actually use metrics behind the important categories and their outcomes. There is an old saying that "what can be measured can be managed." There is something very important to specific work categories that can use metrics. For example, a writer would keep track of the number of words written in a day. In case you are a salesman, you can keep track of how many potential clients you talked to in the month (or just plain how many people you talked to) and how many of those potential clients converted. Whatever is the top priority of your business, try to put metrics behind the priority as much as possible.

4. Prepare Ongoing List. The next item on the list will be to prepare an ongoing list of work items or tasks. You can actually use a WordPad file, which is to be kept open all the time. Every time you perform an activity, write it down. This idea is a bit derived from what you talk about in the DDR (delete, delegate, and redesign) technique. Once you have prepared the ongoing list of all the things you need to on daily, find out the things you can delete. Look for the chores you can delegate, or look for things that can be redesigned or taken off the plate.

These things are to be done constantly. You can take the help of a virtual assistant. You can expect the assistant to take things away from your plate or even look for tasks that can be entirely removed. The best way to find it is to have an ongoing list that you can constantly update. These are some of the things you can do that really help.

Timelogger

Is Timelogger a website or an app for the mobile? It is an app. It can be used on both iOS and Android devices. Most people in the world should be able to reach it. Although it is a paid app, it doesn't cost much. There are other ways to track your time as well. This app is really simple to use and figure out.

80/20 Rule

The writers who practice habit stacking ask their readers to get 1 percent better on each day. Challenges set you off on the habit stacking journey. Another recommendation is the application of 80–20 rule. The idea is to have 80 percent results coming with an effort of 20 percent. The readers need to identify what their 80 percent is and what the 20 percent is. What is the thing that makes a big difference for your career? From there on, track your time spent obsessively. It is quite possible that you may have to do it just for a couple of weeks. However, track the time enthusiastically and find out the ways to eliminate the things that are getting in the way of the 80–20. In case you find that you are spending way too much time on e-mailing, then you need to apply the DDR technique. Try to find out ways to streamline the time spent on the e-mailing so that you may actually manage to spend more time performing the 80–20 tasks.

Just look for ways of improving weekly and then improving that. Most people will like to spend half of their time doing the work, and you need to ruthlessly eliminate the things that get in the way.

Chapter 1: Synaptic Pruning and Habit Stacking

Synaptic Pruning and Habit Stacking

During the year 2007, the researchers at Oxford University started looking inside the brain of newly born human babies. There were surprising results. When they compared the brain of a newborn baby with that of a grown adult, they realized that the average adults have 41 percent lesser neurons than average newborn babies. This discovery did not make sense in the beginning because if the babies have more neurons, how come the adults who are smarter and more skilled have less? Let's check what the case is and why it is important and what it has to do with habit stacking and mastering your physical and mental performance.

Synaptic Pruning

There is an event that happens with humans as they age called as synaptic pruning. Connections between various neurons in the brain are called as synapses. The elementary idea is that the human brain prunes the connection between neurons that are unused and builds connections between those that are used frequently. For example, you practiced a wired instrument for ten years, and then the brain will strengthen the connections between neurons used for the music. The more you play, the stronger will be the connection. Not just that, these connections get faster and more efficient every time you practice. As the brain develops faster and stronger connections between neurons, you become more capable of expressing your skills with ease and expertise. It is the biological change that leads to the development of skills.

At the same time, someone who has not played the wire instrument ever is not developing those connections in the brain and, as a result, the brain prunes out those connections and allocates the energy toward building the connection for other skills in your life. This also explains the difference between adult and newborn baby's brains. Babies come into this world with brains like a blank canvas. Everything is a possibility; however, they do not have developed connections everywhere. Adults, on the other hand, have pruned away a lot of their neurons but have very strong connections, which are good for some skills. Now, let's see the role of synaptic pruning in the development of new habits.

Synaptic Pruning and Building New Habits

Synaptic pruning happens every time you build a new habit. As described above, your brain develops a network of neurons to support your current behavior. The more you perform a certain activity, the more efficient and stronger the connections become. In all probability, you have strong habits and connections that you take for granted every day. For example, the brain is very efficient at remembering the daily chores, such as taking a shower or going to work or even taking a coffee or opening up the blinds once the sun rises. There are thousands of such habits you work on every day. You can take advantage of the strong neural connections to develop new habits. Let's see how.

When you are trying to build new habits, you may use the connections of different behaviors to your advantage. One of the easiest ways of building new habits is by identifying a current habit you already have and use every day and then stack a new one on top of it. This is called habit stacking. It is a special form of what is called an implementation intention. Instead of pairing your new habits with a location or time, you can pair it with current habits. The method developed by B. J. Hogg is a part of his program called Tiny Habits. It can be used to develop a cue for almost all habits.

Examples of Habit Stacking

The formula used for habit stacking is "After/Before [CURRENT HABIT], I will [NEW HABIT]." For example:

- After pouring my coffee in the mug every day, I will meditate for one minute.
- After taking off my shoes after work, I will change into my gym wear immediately.
- After I sit down for my dinner, I will say one thing that suggests that I am grateful for what happened today.
- After I get in bed for the night, I will kiss my partner goodnight.
- After I put on my jogging slacks, I will text a family member informing him where I am going for the run today and how much time it will take.

You need to remember that the reason habit stacking works so beautifully is that the current habits are already present in your brain. The behavior and its pattern that has been strengthened over the years are present in the brain. You are basically linking the new habits to a cycle that is built inside the brain. By doing so, you make it more likely that you will stick to the new habit pattern.

Once this basic structure is mastered, you can start to create large stacks by connecting the smaller habits together. This provides you the advantage of natural momentum, which comes from one behavior leading into the next. So now your routine morning habit stack can look like this:

1. After pouring my coffee in the mug every day, I will meditate for one minute.
2. After meditating for one minute, I write a to-do list for the

day.

3. After writing the to-do list for the day, I will begin my first assignment.

For your evening, habit stack may look like this:

1. After finishing my dinner, I will put my plate in the dishwasher.
2. After putting away the cleaned plates from the dishwasher, I will wipe out the counter immediately.
3. After wiping the counter clean, I will put my coffee mug in its place for tomorrow.

It is also possible to insert new patterns in the middle of the current routines. For instance, your morning routine may look somewhat like this: (1) wake up in the morning, (2) make the bed, and (3) take my shower. Let us say that you wish to develop your reading habit every night and read more. You may expand habit stacks and develop a routine like this: (1) wake up in the morning, (2) make the bed, (3) place a book on the bed, and (4) take my shower. Now when you return to bed every night, a book will be waiting there for your enjoyment.

All in all, habit stacking is a way of creating a set of easy rules that guide your future behavior. It is like having a game plan for all the actions coming up during the day. Once you are comfortable with the approach, you may develop general habit stacks that will guide you when a situation arises. Here are some examples:

1. When I see a set of stairs, I will take them rather than using the elevator.
2. To develop my social skills, when I go to a party, I will acquaint myself to the people I don't know.
3. Whenever I wish to purchase things with a price higher than $100, I will wait for one day before making the buy.

4. To develop healthy eating habits, whenever I serve myself some food, I will always place veggies on the plate first.
5. Every time I purchase some new item, I will give one away (for one in, one goes out).
6. When my phone rings, I will take a deep breath and smile before replying.
7. When I am taking a leave from any public place, I will check my chair and tables to ensure that I have not left anything behind.

It doesn't matter how you make use of the strategy. The secret to creating a fruitful habit stack is the selection of a right cue to set things off. This is unlike implementation intention in which we just specify the time and location for a behavior. Habit stacking has this information implicitly built into it: *when* you decide to insert a habit in your daily routine and *where* it can make a huge difference. In case you are trying to add a meditation routine in your morning but your mornings are too chaotic and the kids are running in and out of the rooms, then that is the wrong time and place to insert meditation. Think of when you are likely to be more successful. Do not ask yourself to develop a habit when you are preoccupied with another chore.

Remember, your cue must have the same frequency as the desired habit you need to insert. In case you are trying to develop a habit each day and you are going to stack it on top of an existing habit, it is probably not a very good choice.

Looking for the Right Trigger

One of the easiest ways of looking for the right trigger for your stack is by brainstorming the list of your current habits. Make use of the habit scorecard as your starting point, or you may create a list having two columns. In the first, write down the habits you have and work on every day without fail. Here are some examples:

- getting out of the bed
- taking shower
- cleaning your teeth
- dressing up
- having a coffee
- having breakfast
- taking your kids to school
- starting at work
- having lunch
- ending the working day
- getting out of the working clothes
- having your dinner
- turning off the lights
- getting in bed

This list could be longer, but now you have the idea. In the second column in front of the habit, write down what happens to you every day without fail. Here are some examples:

- The sun rises.
- You get a phone call.
- The song you were listening to ends.
- The sun sets.

When you are armed with these two lists, you can start searching for the best place to insert the new habit in your lifestyle.

The Next Step

Habit stacking is at its best when the cues are accurate and specific and when they are actionable. Some people select cues that are vague. This mistake is done by the experts as well. For example, when an expert wanted to start his push-up habit, his habit stack was "When I take the lunch break, I will perform ten push-ups." This sounded all right at first, but later he realized that the cue was not clear. Would you do them before you take the lunch or after? Where would you do them? After a few inconsistent days, he changed the habit stack to "When I close the laptop for lunch, I will do ten push-ups immediately next to the desk." This pushed aside the ambiguity from the original cue and made the task realistic and successful as a result.

Habits such as "Eat better" or "Read more" are worthy causes to our lifestyles, but they are very vague. The goals do not provide instructions on when and how to act. You need to be specific and clear like "After I brush my teeth" or "After I close the door" or "After I sit at my table." It is significant to the success of the habit. The more tightly attached the new habit is to the cue, the better are the chances that you will notice it when it is time to act.

Chapter 2: 17 Productivity Habits of Habit Stacking

Mini Habits

The target for a mini habit is to be reliable and consistent. As a matter of fact, it is even more important than the actual achievement by using the daily habit. The idea behind mini habits is that you achieve larger goals (larger habits) if you start small, set easy goals, and aim more at consistency. Stephen Guise has given the example of "The One Push-Up Challenge" in his book *Mini Habits: Small Habits, Bigger Results*. He was feeling exactly like a lot of us do, feeling guilty about many things, such as not working out. He tried to accommodate years of exercise in his first workout, which developed an all-or-nothing attitude, and shifted his focus on goals and not on how we do it. One fine day, he decided to do the opposite and did just a single push-up.

This permitted him to check the box marked for completing the activity. It's just that he didn't stop at one but completed fourteen more. Then he did just the one push-up, and you know what? He didn't stop at one again. The workout went on like this, and when he was all done, it turned out to be a pretty good exercise. Remember, it started with a single push-up.

S. J. Scott writes this in his book *Habit Stacking: 97 Small Life Changes That Take Five Minutes or Less*: "The core idea behind the mini-habits concept is that you can build a major habit by thinking small enough to get started. Most people don't need the motivation to do one push-up, so it's easy to get started. And once you get going, you'll find it's easy to keep at it."

Elements of Habit Stacking

The main purpose of habit stacking is to develop repeatable and simple routines managed by checklists. The reason is to get this outside the cognitive load as you just have to remember to follow a checklist and all your tasks are done. There is no need to remember independent habits. You will do this by performing the same set of actions in the same order and manner every day. The checklists do more than just telling you to perform the next task; they aid you in dealing with the complexity of tasks and increase productivity. Scott says: "Linking habits together is a way of getting more done in less time, resulting in a positive change in your life. As you perform the stacked actions every day, they become part of your daily routine."

As per Scott, there are eight elements in a habit-stacking routine:

1. Every habit takes less than five minutes to finish.
2. It is a complete habit.
3. It must improve your life.
4. It is easy to finish.
5. The entire process must not exceed thirty minutes.
6. It follows a logical thought process.
7. It must follow a defined checklist.
8. It must fit your life pattern.

17 Small Productivity Habits

All the listed habits are from S. J. Scott's book, *Habit Stacking: 97 Small Life Changes That Take Five Minutes or Less*. Although you may not agree with all of them, they are mostly derived out of common sense. Scott says that if you add them to your routine, you will see a dramatic improvement in both the quality and quantity of your efforts. A lot of improvement can be observed just by being aware and being cautious about what you are doing and how you spend your time.

1. Drink one large glass of water. Mildest of dehydration are capable of causing headaches and fatigue. It affects your concentration, impairs the short-term memory, and impedes mental function. In case you wish to be at your productive best, it is important for the brain to be firing all cylinders. Therefore, ensure that you are well hydrated before beginning your work.

2. Schedule and prioritize the daily tasks. Without having a basic schedule in place, it is scarily easy to get to the end of the day and then realize that you have achieved nothing of importance. At least you need to make a list of tasks you wish done during the day and then decide where your priorities are. In case you are lost on how to do this, there is some online help available for it as well.

3. Concentrate on the three most significant tasks. There is another way to plan the day ahead and that is by focusing on the MITs (most important tasks). It is easy to try to do too much in a day. As a result, you get toward the end of the day, and you have not completed the task. Then you feel guilty of not having a successful day. By picking the MITs every day, you don't waste your time on low-priority tasks. In case you manage to complete your MITs, you will feel productive even if you have not done anything else on the list.

4. Convert tasks into manageable steps. For every task on your checklist, try to break it into smaller steps so that the task is easy to manage.

5. Tell others to create accountability. In case your tasks do not have accountability, try to build it into them like having a client deadline. Accountability can be created by telling others about your intentions as it disciplines your efforts of staying on the task. There is no need to embarrass yourself by admitting that you could not get the work done on time. This way, you will be keener to achieve those goals by making the target public.

6. Reward yourself for completing the tasks. In order to keep your energy levels up and morale high, alternate between small tasks, and reward yourself with small treats. The treats not only act as a relief to replenish the depleted focus levels but also work as a carrot on the stick. You will work faster with renewed enthusiasm if you have something to look forward to at the end of the day.

7. Extract distractions from work. Instead of struggling against the brain's natural inclination to procrastinate, save yourself the trouble of losing a lot of money and time by just closing the e-mail tab and stopping the use of social media during work time.

8. Clear the desktop. Complete all the paperwork from your desk except for what you will need for the remaining day. Place everything else in physical folders, boxes, and drawers out of sight and hopefully out of your mind.

9. Use white noise or play music to increase focus. Low-level music at the background helps in muffling the distracting sounds that may interrupt your work, and this has proved to be capable of improving creativity and focus of several people.

10. Complete the most difficult (or appalling) task first. Take a look at the MITs and find the most appalling task for the day, the kind that you will put off indefinitely if given the chance. Start working on this task first before you had the chance to think about it. Do not touch other work until you are done with this task.

11. Commit just to a small goal. Identify your hardest task and plan a small first and simple step toward completing it. It may take just a few minutes. Decide a metric you can easily use to complete assessment of the data on the task.

12. Work in small blocks at a time. You can use the Pomodoro technique as it is the most well-known version of the technique. It means working for twenty-five minutes and then taking a five-minute break.

13. Keep track of time required for various activities. Most people misjudge the amount of time they are using up doing the actual task and spend a surprisingly large amount of time doing mindless tasks. By tracking your time, you become more alert about how you are spending it, and you can begin spotting patterns in your schedule that are decreasing your productivity.

14. Use the two-minute rule. In case there is a task that will take around two minutes of your time or less, deal with it and move on immediately. Keep in mind that the urgent always trumps over the meaningful.

15. Capture all ideas. Our minds have a tendency to wander. Despite heroic efforts, sometimes they drift away from the task at hand. Instead of this being the drawback, it is a fascinating way of gaining insights. Pull out a paper and a pen and write down all the ideas. You can come back to the ideas later, and who knows, there might be a great one you were always looking for or a solution to an issue you have been facing for a long time.

16. Write down a completed-assignment (done) list. A lot of people are familiar with to-do lists. However, these lists can make you feel overwhelmed and demoralized as a result if you stuff too much into them. The done list, on the other hand, provides the balancing effect. By writing down everything you have completed during the day, you will feel motivated for continuation.

17. Review the target. Everyone has a target or goals. Whether these goals are small or big, we all have targets we wish to accomplish. However, the hustle and bustle of daily life sometimes make you go off the boil. So you need to review your goals and create plans for reaching those goals, placing your day into perspective and knowing what is important.

Chapter 3: Train the Brain for Routine

Habit stacking is fine, but how do you train your brain to accept the routine? The answer is to get the tasks done by grouping together the assignments in pattern chains. Let us check out a strategy that will turn a nagging to-do list into an unconscious act. As we grow older, we prune the synapses for behaviors that are not in use anymore, and we strengthen the ones that are in use. Habit stacking utilizes strong connections to develop new habits.

We are what we repeatedly do. This makes excellence not just an act but a habit. That's what Aristotle used to say. Great words from a great person, but try putting that into practice at 7:00 a.m. when you are hitting the snooze period or you are watching lashing rains from your office windows at 5:00 p.m. and are firmly parking any possibilities of an early exit.

However, sometimes the small and niggling tasks linger on the to-do list, and they become a habit that is as natural as brushing your teeth or putting on the socks. Where do we find answers to that? This phrase *habit stacking* was framed by S. J. Scott, who is a bestselling author of *Wall Street Journal*. The book he wrote in 2014 called *Habit Stacking: 97 Small Life Changes That Take Five Minutes or Less* claims that you need to build routines around the habits that do not need effort. The reason being small wins build momentum toward greater achievements as they are easy to complete and remember.

Habit stacking is also termed as *habit chaining* sometimes. You are required to group together small activities and develop a routine that is then linked to a habit already set in the day. This results in making the routine memorable and anchors the new habits to existing triggers. Or in simple words, use the things you already remember to remind you to perform some other task, like reading just a single chapter of a book when you are in bed.

This strategy works as it eliminates procrastination and in its place makes a practical routine out of things you used to put off. You never remembered to floss after washing your mouth? Work it inside existing habits by saying flossing before brushing the teeth. Assuming you are remembering the original activity, that is. Otherwise, place it in the checklist discussed in the earlier chapters.

Synaptic pruning is happening with every habit you pick up or build as the brain builds a solid network of neurons to support your existing behavior. The more you do something, the more efficient and stronger your neural connections become. James Clear argues that you take advantage of the strong habits and connections that you take for granted every day for building new habits. In case all that sounds difficult, try to break down the habits in small five-minute chunks. This allows you to complete multiple assignments each day, and during the week, it adds up to a time of half an hour. For example, a habit stack may look like this:

- Wake up in the morning.
- Five minutes of meditation.
- Take vitamin pills.
- Five minutes of abdominal exercises.
- Brush your teeth.
- Floss.
- Make breakfast.
- Empty laundry bin into the washing machine.
- Call mother during the walk to tube.

Did you get the picture? And in case if you are not a morning person, don't worry. It is not the list you need to master in the beginning. Scott recommends that you create stacks for the last few minutes of work, which will set you up for the upcoming morning. Or you may compile a twenty-minute habit chain as you arrive back home to be able to tick off the things on the checklist, such as wardrobe or meal planning.

Scott also suggested that you make an exercise stack that will give you an efficient and condensed workout, thereby making the exercise less daunting. Although making a commitment to a half-an-hour run might seem implausible, twenty minutes with getting five things done is definitely plausible. Research has made it clear that it takes twenty-one to forty days to develop a habit, so what looks like unachievable and jumbled now can be your morning routine within a span of three weeks. Refer to Aristotle if you have any doubts.

Chapter 4: Building a Habit-Stacking Routine: 13 Easy Steps

We are all aware that it is not easy to add several new habits to your daily routine. However, what you may not realize is that it is fairly easy to build a single routine that is new. Read on for some steps to turn the small positive habits into an easy-to-complete sequence of tasks. Habit stacking is nothing but a strategy that can be used to group together little changes in a single routine that can be followed daily.

The secret to consistency is to treat the habit stack as a single action rather than a series of independent tasks. This may seem like a simple thing, but building habits need several elements if you wish the habits to stick. Here are some examples:

- scheduling time for a task (one block of time)
- identifying the trigger
- planning what you will do to finish the action

The point is, in case you treated every component of a stack as an independent action, then you will also need to have a reminder in place and track every behavior that can be overwhelmingly fast. But if you treat the whole routine as a single habit, then it becomes easier to remember and complete consistently. Habit stacking is overwhelming initially, but once you start and do it a few times, it is not as hard. The key is to start with little expectations and then build the muscle memory for completing the routine, and then add more tasks to the routine when you have become consistent. We will see how to do that now.

What you are about to find out is a proven process for building some permanent habit stacks. It is a simple and straightforward process that will not leave you feeling overwhelmed. In case you closely follow and finish the steps, you will discover that you will develop lasting changes in your life. Let us see them:

Step 1: Begin with one 5-minute block. The easiest way of sticking to a new habit is to make it stupidly simple and easy to complete. This is a valuable lesson to be learned from the Stephen Guise book *Mini Habits*. For example, if you wish to write each day, then you make a rule that you will write just a single paragraph every day. Sure, you can do a lot more than that, but as long as you have finished the task, you can consider it as a completed task for the day. The basic idea is to set easy-to-achieve goals that will overcome inertia. Then as you get started, you will start performing better and doing more work than initially planned.

It is strongly recommended to apply mini habits to the stacks. In the beginning, the single most important factor is consistency. This is the reason why you need to start with five minutes in which you pick just one or two habits and then add more as the routine becomes an automatic process. Some people might feel this is not enough to accomplish anything big. Read on, and you will discover that the eleven habit stack detailed in the chapter exemplifies four habits that take just five minutes to complete. Not bad, right, for a shrunk block of time? Apart from this, there are dozens of habits beginning in later parts of the chapter that takes only a minute or two. So although a five-minute stack may not appear like much, you will be amazed at how much activity can be fitted into such a short period.

Step 2: Concentrate on small and easy wins. Always build your routine with habits that do not require much effort. These small wins will build emotional momentum as they are easy to remember and finish. By small wins are actions that do not need much willpower. For example, taking vitamin pills, weighing yourself, filling a bottle of water for work, or just reviewing your goals. Yes, they are incredibly simple tasks, but that is the point. You should get started with these activities that really do not need any brains. They will eliminate the chances that you will skip a day because you are overwhelmed or are generally busy. You can find the seven-goal categories in part 2 of Scott's book. You can find actions that are easy to complete, like those that need less than two minutes to finish, then build your stack around these actions. Focus on these tasks for a week or two until it is automatic. Only after this should you add habits to the routine.

Step 3: Pick location and time. Each habit stack needs to anchor to a trigger, which is related to a time of the day, location, or a combination of both. Let's see some actions that can be used as cues for completing specific stacks.

- **At home in the morning.** Finishing the morning routine as soon as you can ensure that you start the day in a great manner as you will start in an energetic manner. You may finish a series of activities from a stack that will have a positive impact on your life. This energy carries over onto the more significant tasks, which will mark the beginning of the workday. These small habits could be meditation, reviewing the goals, reciting affirmations, reading nonfiction books, or drinking a nutritious juice/shake.

- **In the morning at work.** When you go to the office every morning, instead of just checking the e-mail or social media calls like most people, maximize the first period by creating an environment that allows you to focus on the high-level tasks. The smaller tasks include identifying the top three priority tasks of the day, deciding the next steps of your high-priority projects, removing unwanted distractions, and then starting your day with the hardest task of the day.

- **In the lunch break at work.** Lunch break is approximately the middle of the workday and is a great time to finish a stack. You have worked for a few hours and, as a result, are feeling a reduction in energy levels. The best way to overcome the negative state is by eating a quick lunch at the desk (just before or after the stack) and then complete the stacks that will prepare you for the rest of the afternoon. These small habits may be meditation, taking a walk, getting a small seven-minute workout, calling for an accountability partner, or finishing an exercise at the desk routine.

- **At the end of the workday at work.** The last minutes of the workday is a perfect period for completing a stack as it sets you up for a win the next day when you come to work or after the weekend. You have been working all day, so with the end of the daily routine, you can leave feeling positive about what you have managed during the day. These small habits could be writing a journal, identifying the important work from tomorrow, or tracking the amount of time you spent on every activity of the day.

- **Early in the evening at home.** You may squeeze in a heap between when you are reaching the home and before you go to bed. As a matter of fact, this is a perfect opportunity to work on those personal and small things that are important to you but have never been urgent enough to demand attention. These small habits could be practicing some skill, reviewing your expenses, planning meals for the week, or reorganizing certain areas of your home.

- **At the gym or at the place you exercise.** Yes, you may add stacks even to the exercise routines. As a matter of fact, creating a routine for the workout will aid you in completing the important exercises in a short period. Although exercising is not a stack commodity, there are several habits that can help you with the activity. These are drinking a health supplement, stretching, weighing yourself, recording metrics from the workout stats, or creating a playlist with your favorite songs or podcasts.

Step 4: Anchoring the Stack to a Trigger. This word *trigger* has many meanings for many people. In this case, the definition of *trigger* is a cue that makes use of one of the five senses (sound, sight, smell, taste, or touch) to act as a reminder in order to complete specific actions. The triggers are important because most persons do not remember a huge number of tasks without any reminders. So the trigger can push you toward taking actions. For example, several people make use of alarm clocks or mobile phones as a trigger to wake them in the mornings.

There are two basic kinds of triggers. The first is an external trigger, like push notification or a cell phone alarm or a Post-it note on the fridge. The external triggers are successful because they develop a Pavlovian response that when, say, an alarm goes off, you will complete a specific activity. The second kind of trigger is the internal trigger. The examples of internal triggers include thoughts, feelings, and emotions that you associate with established habits. They are like an itch you need to scratch.

For example, in case you have ever felt the need to check in with social media, this is an action as a result of internal triggers. It is important to understand the difference between the two triggers because not only will it help you build strong habit stacks but also it will help in overcoming the negative habits that might be restricting your growth as a human being. Let's see a negative example.

Habit Triggers (Negative Example)

As we are all aware, there are several popular social media websites, such as Twitter, Facebook, Instagram, and Pinterest. You either love them or hate them, but they have become a ubiquitous part of the modern culture. But how did these sites become so popular? The brains behind the sites understand how the human mind works. So they have designed the system to hook the users permanently and asking for more.

In case you have been to any of the social media sites, then you have probably noticed that they use alerts for all kinds of behavior. When someone comments, tweets, likes, or shares something you posted, you will get a notification. These are visual or auditory cues or sometimes both. A signal goes off in the brain, and your respond similar to one of Pavlov's dogs.

The triggers can get addictive as they act as a reward for posting content that the public likes. As a matter of fact, at one point, you have logged into a social media website just to check out what your friends think of a post you have updated. This constant exposure to notifications creates a habit loop that is discussed by Charles Duhigg in his book *The Power of Habit*. It is broken into three actions:

- *Cue.* This is the auditory or visual reminder to use a social media website.
- *Routine.* The pattern you need to follow for checking in (opening the app or clicking to the site).
- *Reward.* The psychological pleasure you get by using the site (for example, because of the fact that someone like your post).

These triggers can also be negative when they are responsible for permanent behavior, such as when you feel a compulsive need for checking a site several times daily. As a matter of fact, without getting prompted as in case you are bored, you will feel an unconscious desire to open the browser and go to the social site without even realizing that you are addicted to it.

This happens to be a classical example of internal triggers. Due to the constant exposure to the social sites, you develop a permanent habit. When you are distracted or bored, you can have a quick dopamine rush by visiting your loved social website. What generally happens is what you thought will be just a few minutes turns out to be thirty minutes or more of a lot of wasted time.

The tech organizations use external triggers all the while to create and develop these internal triggers. This is how they are building their pool of loyal clients. They are well aware that repeated exposure to external cues will increase their overall use, especially when their product is an escape from an otherwise tiring and boring day. Eventually, the users access their products when they are feeling unmotivated.

So when any product is providing a positive experience (for example, a budgeting app, such as Mint), then it is developed to build good habits. However, if some product is turning out to be harmful, such as addictive video games, then it is developed to build bad habits. You can read a book called *Hooked* by Nir Eyal for a detailed explanation of how technology is designed to increase addictive behavior and what can be done to identify these patterns in your everyday life and remove the patterns.

You need to remember that there is something important to be learned about triggers. As a matter of fact, this knowledge can be used to build positive habits in your life. So let's see the positive example of triggers.

Habit Triggers (Positive Example)

It is recommended that you create a trigger for every habit-stacking routine. For example, put the dental floss in some obvious location inside your bathroom, possibly just next to the toothbrush. This will act as a visual reminder for using the floss after brushing your teeth. It could be before or after brushing the teeth. This is just one example of triggers. In case you are creating triggers for the habit stacks, then it is recommended that you keep four things in your mind:

1. The trigger must be an existing habit. It has to be an action you perform automatically every day, like brushing your teeth, showering, going to the fridge, checking the mobile phone, or sitting at the desk. This is so significant because you have to be 100 percent sure that you will not miss the reminder.

2. A specific time of the day can be the trigger. The reminder for any habit can also be a specific time of the day, such as the time when you wake up in the morning or when you take your lunch or even walking away from the office after completing daily work. Again, whichever time you select, it has to be an automatic habit of yours.

3. The trigger must be easy to complete. In the event the action is challenging, although you perform the action every day, you are decreasing the effectiveness of the trigger. For example, even though you exercise daily, it is a mistake to use it as the trigger as you are likely to miss out on odd occasions.

4. The trigger must not be a new habit. It takes from twenty-one to sixty-six days to develop permanent habits. Many times, it is even longer for the ones that are very challenging. Therefore, you need not pick new habits as triggers as you are not 100 percent sure that you will do the thing daily consistently.

These are just some of the thumb rules for picking triggers. In order to simplify things even further, it is recommended that you pick up some of the following habits as you, in all probability, do them daily:

- brushing your teeth
- having your breakfast
- having your lunch
- having your dinner
- getting inside your car for going to work
- arriving at the office or place of employment
- starting your desktop/laptop in the morning
- leaving the place of your office
- walking inside the house after coming back from work
- creating a mobile phone alarm for a specific time
- keeping visual reminders in key locations, like your desktop, TV, or fridge

As you may observe, there are many kinds of triggers that can act as reminders for the stack. Actually, the easiest method for picking one is to match trigger with the first habit of the stack. The idea here is to develop a trigger that pushes you into action, and then you can use the checklist to navigate through the rest of the small activities. So let's go and see what is next.

Step 5: Create Logical Checklists. Checklists are the most significant parts of any stacks. It must include the series of actions, how long it will take to complete each activity, and where you will do them. It is admitted that it's a little obsessive to have all this information; however, it will remove all the guesswork about what is required to complete specific actions. We have discussed checklists previously, so we will not waste time rehashing them again. It suffices to mention that you need to put the small actions together in a way that they flow effortlessly with each other and there is no wastage.

Step 6: Accountability. Most people would have heard about the law of inertia. It is also known as Newton's first law of motion. Here, it is in case you have not heard about it: "An object at rest stays at rest, and an object in motion stays in motion with the same speed and in the same direction unless acted upon by an unbalanced force." In other words, in case your natural tendency is to hang around before starting your day, you need an additional push to get you in action. Most people often fail to build habits as it is a lot easier to rest than it is to do something creative and potentially unpleasant. As a matter of fact, the biggest thing to understand is that you must have accountability to stick to major goals.

It is not enough to make personal commitments. The big achievements in life need a solid action plan and a support network to tap into when obstacles are met. This is also true in the world of business and for personal development. If you have someone who will cheer you on or kick you in the butt if you are not performing, you are less likely to give up. There are a number of methods to be accountable, such as posting your progress on the social sites, telling people close to you about the new routines, or even punishing yourselves for not staying focused on goals by using apps such as Beeminder.

There are two techniques that can be used for building new habits. The first is Coach.me. It is a fantastic tool for maintaining and sticking to new habits. It is similar to having a coach in your pockets both for good and bad. You will be held accountable for your habit-stacking routine with the addition of habits and verifying every day whether the habit has been completed. The very fact that you have to update people about the progress you are making about a certain task is a motivation enough to complete the habit-stacking routine.

The second technique is having an accountability partner. You can share your challenges, breakthroughs, and future plans with him. This, in fact, is a great method to get a kick in the behind when you feel that you are waning in motivation. You will have someone you can confide in when there is a challenge that warrantees second opinion. In case you are looking to find such accountability partners, then be sure to look into a Facebook group called HabitsGroup.com. It has more than one thousand members. Each month, they create a thread in which members can connect with each other and eventually become accountability partners.

Step 7: Make Small and Enjoyable Rewards. Completing the habit-stacking routine can be termed as an achievement, and so it must be rewarded. Allowing yourselves a reward for the achievement is a great motivator for finishing the daily routine. This includes anything from watching your favorite TV shows, eating healthy snacks, or even relaxing for some time. Actually, the reward can be anything that you enjoy doing frequently. The only piece of advice here is that you should avoid rewards that will eliminate the benefit achieved through a certain habit. For example, in case you have just completed small actions to lose weight, then your reward cannot be a 400-calorie chocolate cake as it defeats the achievement of the stack, right? There are several things you can reward yourself with. For some ideas, you can read some of the blog posts here: https://www.developgoodhabits.com/reward-yourself/.

Step 8: Concentrate on Repetition. Repetition is key during the first few weeks while building a stack. It is critical that you stick to a routine even when you are sometimes forced to skip one or two of your activities. Consistency is more critical than anything as repetition builds your muscle memory. And when you finish the various routines often, they become an integral part of your day, such as brushing your teeth.

Having said all that, it is not the end of the world if you miss the routine on occasional days. It can happen to the best of us. However, you should never miss two days in a row. This creates a slippery passage, and it becomes progressively easier to miss more days. If you miss often, it is a certainty that you will give up the routine after a point of time. This, by the way, leads to another bit of advice.

Step 9: Do Not Break the Chain. There are many stories about habits floating around. One of the most interesting ones come from the popular comedian Jerry Seinfeld. While talking to a new comedian, Seinfeld gave simple advice—set some time aside every day to develop new material. The key is to not miss a single day even when you are not in the mood. This is at the risk of sounding familiar.

At the beginning of a year, Seinfeld hangs a calendar on the wall and makes a huge X on it every time he writes new comic stuff. There is no need to write a lot each day. What is more important is that there is something each day without fail. He is completely focused on not breaking the chain. By making the X marks on the calendar, he is encouraging himself to complete desired tasks every single day. As the unbroken string of X marks grows on the calendar, you will feel more compulsion toward getting over the initial resistance and forcing yourself to get going.

The reason behind not breaking the chain is to eliminate the excuses. Many times it is easy to envisage creative reasons for not getting started on a stack. You are busy, tired, sick, overwhelmed, hung over, or depressed. All these are valid reasons for skipping the routine. However, in case you keep missing the routine on the following days, it becomes a reason for missing it whenever you feel like it.

The advice here is simple. Create a practical daily target that can be achieved no matter what, and do not allow yourself to talk out of it. It is possible that you will end up setting smaller goals that you can achieve in two or three actions. The important part is to set goals that can be achieved even when you are having an off day.

Step 10: Pretty Much Expect Some Setbacks. You can expect some setbacks or challenges even for the most consistent of habits. As a matter of fact, when you have done something for a very long time, it is guaranteed that there will be times when you will receive unexpected setbacks. For example, the writer Scott has been a runner since 1990. If you do the math, you will be looking at twenty-eight years of distance running. In almost thirty years of the exercise habit, he has experienced a range of setbacks, including boredom, weird illnesses, multiple injuries, dog attacks, pedestrian incidences, and life-threatening car accidents.

As you may very well imagine, these incidents have put forward a challenge for the daily routine and especially the consistency part of the routine having just a single habit. However, the bestselling author says it has taught him the significance of resilience and sticking to something although you are experiencing setbacks. He will go as far as saying that setbacks are good because they teach you resilience and help you in becoming nonfragile. This is discussed in details by Nassim Taleb in his book called *Antifragile*.

The bottom line is that you can expect challenges to rise due to the routine. Whenever they do, you will have one of the two choices: give up or find a way to overcome the challenges. Hopefully, you will try to look to overcome the challenges. If you do so, it is recommended that you check chapter 12 of Scott's book.

Step 11: Scheduling the Stack Frequency. As described earlier, some stacks are required to be completed on an irregular basis—daily, weekly, or monthly. In the beginning, you need to start with small daily habits. However, as you become comfortable with strategy, it is recommended that you create separate stacks for daily, monthly, or weekly targets.

These stacks should ideally be check-in habits, which you know are significant but are too easy to forget, such as reviewing the credit card statements, planning your fun activities, or completing the safety checks. By placing them in routinely scheduled activities, you will ensure that these tasks are finished without having them weighing on your conscious as yet another activity you have not completed.

Step 12: Scaling Up the Stacks. Go back to the first step of the procedure. Begin with just a five-minute block. In case you can provide just a limited amount of time to a certain stack, then it is not possible to get value out of it. That is why it is recommended that you build a thirty-minute stack eventually, which can contain six 5-minute blocks. Do this with incremental manner. In the first week, the routine will last only five minutes. The second week, it will go on for ten minutes. Then it will be fifteen minutes for the third. Keep repeating the process until the routine is thirty minutes having a handful of little actions.

This scaling up does not mean that you haphazardly add a roll of small habits in the routine. Rather, you need to ensure that you are consistently finishing the routine and not expecting any resistance to the activity. Do not ignore the feelings of being bored, stressed, or overwhelmed when related to the stacks. In case you notice it is getting progressively difficult to get started (for example, when you are procrastinating), then it is time to either reduce the blocks or start asking yourselves the question why you wish to skip a day. The more you understand about lack of motivation, the easier it is to overcome it.

Step 13: Build one stack at a time. One of the biggest habit related to debate is how long it takes to build permanent habits. A lot of people say it will take twenty-one days, and others will say that it takes a few months. As a matter of fact, in research published in the *European Journal of Social Psychology*, it was established by Philippa Lally that it takes some time between 18 to 254 days for some action to become a permanent habit with an average of 66 days. The thing to remember is that you should not try to build more than one habit at a time as every new addition will make it more difficult to stick with the existing stack.

Actually, the only time you even consider adding a new habit is when you stop thinking of habits as habits. Rather, it is just what you do each day without any thought of how and why you are performing the activity. Once you realize that the existing stack has become a permanent behavior, then what you can do is add new habits to the daily routine. There is no recommended timeline for this. Rather, the answer will vary from person to person.

There you are—thirteen steps to build a successful habit-stacking routine. In case you follow these steps, you will be able to identify the significant small actions and place them in a logical framework and then finish them one by one with single triggers or cues.

Chapter 5: Planning Fallacy and Its Effects on Time Management

Let's learn about planning fallacy and how it derails your time management efforts. There are many a time when you will find yourselves racing through work at the last minute for meeting the deadline. Do you often realize that you end up completing projects after the promised date has expired? Have you let down people because there just isn't enough time to fulfill all your obligations? Do all these queries sound familiar? If they do, then you have become a victim of planning fallacy mind-set, and you are probably not even aware of it. Now we will see what planning fallacy is and tell you about the ways to recognize it. We will also see the ways to overcome it and achieve your goals.

What Is It?

Planning fallacy is a universal phenomenon and one of the most consistently demonstrated cognitive bias people have. In case you underestimate the amount of time required for completing a project you are working on or complete packing before going on trips, then you have fallen in the trap of planning fallacy. However, it is a common misconception that planning fallacy just refers to one's tendency to underestimate the time. It also refers to cost and the risk factor to be taken into account when you are doing something even though you have the prior knowledge or experience of doing things required for the given task. It refers to the overly optimistic plans that are unreasonably close to the best-case scenarios.

The fallacy was first proposed by Amos Tversky and Daniel Kahneman in the year 1977. In their research paper, they explained the planning fallacy results from the inclination to ignore the available distributional data and predicting the project outcome based on specific elements of someone's plans. The internal approach to the evaluation of anyone's planning tends to result in underestimation of the plans. For example, a house can be built in the estimated time only if there are no material delay dates, no hazardous weather condition, no employer absence, etc. Although all the hurdles are unlikely to occur, there is all probability that at least one of them will occur. But people do not consider these what-ifs, and this is the reason why they underestimate the task at hand at times. A more reasonable way is to set a proper schedule for a project by asking yourself, "How long did projects like these take in the past?"

Impact of Planning Fallacy on Time Management

Underestimating the time required to finish certain tasks affects the way we manage timing. This, if not done accurately, can negate your plans. This can easily start to get complex with every small task. In case you have five small tasks that you need to complete for finishing a project and you underestimate the time required for completing each task, it is more than likely that completion of the project will be delayed a great deal.

Although it is great to be optimistic and good quality to have most of the time when you are estimating the time requirements for finishing tasks, the optimistic estimates can cause trouble. People often misjudge the time required for finishing a task and undermine the amount of time required to do the task.

People often tend to procrastinate when they think they have quite a bit of time to finish certain assignments of a project and then, as a result, tend to make excuses in the end. It is a standard habit for people to put off tasks they need to do till the last moment. There are reasons for it as there are several distractions or inability to resist things that feel like chores. Either way, in case you are trying to manage time usefully, it is significant that you stay on schedule. Permitting for unplanned contingencies and recognizing the optimistic bias while considering the timeframes will help in stopping us from procrastinating.

Avoid the Planning Fallacy Mind-Set

1. Recognize the fact that everyone is susceptible to planning fallacy, including you: Everybody falls in the planning fallacy trap at some point in time. Make predictions about future work is something everyone does every day. You need to estimate everything from completing the routine aspects around the house to when a large project will finish for an important client. Take these things into consideration while prioritizing and planning the tasks and scheduling your activities.

2. Take the "outsider" view toward the project and find out the time it took the last time you completed a similar task: Always be honest about it. People do not like to remember the difficulties they faced in the previous projects, but you do not want to repeat the mistakes, do you? So you must remember the problems and obstacles you ran into in the past while completing the tasks in hand. Also, note how far behind these obstacles set you. Anyway, for future reference, it is a good idea to track your time while doing things you know you will be required to do again. This will help you have a more realistic estimate of the time required for specific tasks. Remember to keep the optimism in check, and it will help you manage the expectations for the productivity.

3. Consider the time required and the place where you need to complete the activity: By doing this, you will define your activities. After this, you can incorporate all the info you are aware of into the planning process. Thinks about the problems that were presented in the time and place you decided. For example, you are meeting some people for completing a project for the central library. Because of a large number of people also being in that same place, you will need to allow time for their parking, finding the right area in the library for working without distractions, and the possibility of people getting late because of traffic.

4. Take into account the unexpected issues or complications: The unexpected problems do not necessarily mean that your project will get totally derailed. However, you will be required to change the strategy or planning in some manner that will accommodate the issue. Brainstorm at least three possible problems before allotting a time frame to the projected deadline. You must take into account that obstacles will occur in a project.

5. Unpack the tasks: While you are making predictions, remember to pay minute attention to the steps you will be needed to take and not just the outcome of the tasks. Think about every component that is involved in the process and provide sufficient time for it to complete. This will make you aware of everything you need to do to complete the project, including the seemingly trivial things that take up time in the earlier stages and you might forget to consider.

6. Estimate the project completion time in weeks rather than days for the longer and larger assignments: By doing this, you are allowing yourself some cushion for the unexpected things that may come up. In case you estimate the time in days and you are unable to work on a single day, your whole planning gets pushed back. However, when you have allowed yourself an entire week for completing one or two components of the project, you will have much more clemency toward the issues that crop up.

7. Keep some time for the factors that affect and amplify planning fallacy: One of the factors is "incentives." You will promise to finish something quickly in the expectation of a reward. Let's say that there is a financial bonus for you in case you finish the project on a certain date, which is unreasonably short of the actual time frame needed. With the added financial motivation, you will agree to a shortened deadline, thinking that you will find a way of getting it done. However, this turns out to be a false assumption as you are not thinking about all the steps needed in the process.

There is another factor which is "social." You could be trying to impress your boss or an important client by completing a project very fast, causing you to provide an overly optimistic deadline. Although it is extremely tempting to do so, it causes more trouble than benefit in the long run.

8. Use time-motion words rather than ego-motion words while giving instructions to yourself or the others: For example, use a sentence "You just have three hours to finish this task" rather than "You still have three hours to finish the task." As you can see, the former sentence develops a sense of urgency instead of making it sound as if there is an indefinite timeline. Ensure that it is realized that the deadline is finite and is impending. Another example is "As the vacation approaches . . ." rather than "As we approach the vacation . . ." This takes the idea of being in control out of the equation. Although you may feel like you are in control of how you approach the holidays, in case you think of it as if the holiday is approaching you, it turns into something you cannot slow down or stop.

9. Use time management techniques, such as Pomodoro technique, to keep you focused: Getting a time management technique that works out for you helps in becoming more productive. This will improve your chances of actually hitting a deadline. For example, the Pomodoro technique suggests that you should work very focused for short periods and then take breaks. Therefore, after working for twenty-five minutes and placing full attention on the task at hand, you will relent for five minutes and do some stretching. These sessions of deep work help you to stay focused, especially because you are aware at the back of your mind that there is a short break coming up to relax. You can address something that is happening when you concentrate on work.

10. Use programs and technology to your advantage: In case you can raise the velocity of doing some work without sacrificing finesse, go for it. Although the technology is known to slow down people as it can be a distraction, there are some great tools offered by technology for helping you get the work done.

a. Scheduling tools offered by social media: There are many tools you can download from the internet to aid you in organizing the social media in a way that will help you in getting through it quickly. You may have your comments managed simply or set aside some important things you may wish to read later. You might use an app to sort through the posts by topics so that you can discern what you read.

b. Learn quickly using Blinklist: This is an app that provides quick summaries of nonfiction books so there is no need to read the whole thing. You can go through the blinks that only include the most valuable insights provided by the book. They can save you time and money both.

Conclusion

So is the planning fallacy slowing you down? Well, falling into the mind-set of planning fallacy will definitely slow your progress toward achieving your career or personal goals. In case you are able to identify and address this issue before it got out of hand, you are less likely to permit it to influence your success. The reality is that no one wants to be identified as a person who is continuously late or someone who constantly breaks his promises.

Although it is very important to be confident about yourself and your capabilities, it is also significant to be realistic. Stay confident and optimistic about your performance, but do not go overboard by trying to spread yourself thin. The next time you are asked how long it will take to do some work, try to emulate the strategies mentioned above before answering the question as you will be able to provide a correct prediction about the time required for completing the assignment.

Chapter 6: Keystone Habits

In this section, we will see what the keystone habits are and how they build great routines. Why are the keystone habits the most important habits you can develop? They lead to the creation of several good habits. They are responsible for starting a chain effect in your life that produces a lot of positive outcomes. For example, let's say your keystone habit is sleeping eight hours daily at night. The initial goal is to have more sleep, but this can lead to unintended positive outcomes such as the following:

- turning out to be more productive every day
- reduction in the consumption of junk food
- more time for exercise
- better communication with your partner as you are not cranky

In the beginning, you wished for more sleep, but this keystone habit developed a number of habits. The developments from the keystone habits have the potential to become a crucial part of your personal development journey. Let's talk about incorporating this technique into your lifestyle. Let's see a lesson from Charles Duhigg. You will learn a lot about keystone habits from his book titled *The Power of Habit: Why We Do What We Do in Life and Business*. In the book, he talks about developing keystone habits to achieve whatever you wish in your life. There is no need to change a dozen habits to achieve your goals. You just need to change some keystone habits that will produce a ripple effect on the outcomes.

Now let's see how the keystone habits help you. The perfect example is the everyday exercise habit. If you wish to begin exercising for twenty to thirty minutes daily, just this one good habit can lead to several other great habits, like eating healthy food, becoming more efficient at work, or avoiding junk food. This is because you need that extra hour to put in the workout. This single exercise habit can create major breakthroughs in other sections of your life. You begin with a single goal that causes the development of other habits. Here are some additional keystone habits that can lead to major breakthroughs in your life:

1. Eliminating the negative self-talk: Let's see how you can stop your negative self-talk. It can lead to several positive effects in your life. Once you stop talking negatively, you will begin to talk positively. There are many books available even online to develop a positive attitude.

2. Take a leave from the perfectionist mind-set: Removal of the perfectionist mind-set aids you in opening up and experiencing new things. If you are a perfectionist, you don't do many things due to the fear of failure. It makes it difficult to move forward with your aspirations and dreams. When you stop the habit, it allows you to explore the opportunities more, and then you start taking steps toward what you really want. There are many mind-changing books available as well on the internet.

3. Remove the habit of giving excuses: The things that you really wished for in life will not fall in your lap by themselves. You need to stop making excuses for getting the things you wish for in your time. When you stop this habit, it will affect other aspects of your life as you stop making excuses for the lack of results. It is a major breakthrough as you will start to focus on achieving positive outcomes. Read the personal development books for more.

4. Save money: Having saved money will ensure that you have emergency funds for any unforeseen events. This can lead to a lifestyle that is more conscious of expenditure for you and your family. By saving money, you will you pay greater attention to the trivial expenditure you will make in your life. Pretty often this will end up in the reduction in the clutter in your life. You can develop some great financial habits in the process.

Importance of Keystone Habits

They are effective because they concentrate on making dynamic changes in your life. It is like producing a trickle-down effect. Soon you will see more opportunities for self-improvement from the keystone habits that you are forming. Success by using the keystone habits happens when you are taking the first steps. In the beginning, make a list of all the habits you wish to develop. Pay attention to those that can add a ripple effect to your life. Then concentrate on developing the habit over a period of the next thirty days. You will be surprised at how the small changes can generate several positive outcomes.

Chapter 7: Breaking Bad Habits

Here are the steps you can take to break your bad habits and quit the addictions without having the craving pangs. Habits rule our day-to-day lives. Almost everything you do is based on habits you have developed at some point in time in your life. Some of them are useful, but others work against you. What is even worse is that some of the bad habits will have a negative long-term impact on your capability to lead a fulfilling life. Eating junk food, smoking, hoarding, or consuming too much alcohol are all bad habits. Even spending too much time on the net is bad. We all would like to break these habits. Fortunately, it is possible to eliminate negative routines as all you need is a plan of action in place. Here are some strategies to ensure that you break those habits. You will learn how to get rid of bad habits in four phases:

1. planning for a habit change
2. understanding the habit loop/forming new habits
3. building support systems
4. overcoming the challenges

All these strategies build on one another. When you are through reading the chapter, you should pick your worst habit and then create a plan for overcoming the habit. Let's see the first phase:

Phase 1: Planning for the Habit Change

Before actually doing anything you need to prepare for the habit change, chances are that you tried to break this habit in the past and failed as you did not have a plan and relied mostly on the willpower. If you have failed in the past, it doesn't mean that you will fail in the future as well. Normally, it is a direct result of not having solid strategies to break the habit. In other words, the age-old adage was not followed by you: "When you fail to plan, you plan to fail." Therefore, before doing anything, you need to implement these strategies and ensure that you are in the position for success.

Strategy 1: Concentrate on a Single Habit at a Time

There is a term in psychology called *ego depletion*, and it means that your willpower has a small amount of energy each day. When it is stretched, it becomes difficult to control the impulses. Willpower in a way is like a muscle. It can become tired and worn out with a lot of use. In case your days are full of stress and continuous battles to control emotions or thinking, then you will not have the capability to resist temptations. Does it affect habit development? How?

It is straightforward. If you tried to change many habits at the same time, you would not succeed. Every habit requires a certain amount of willpower to resist, and as a result, you will be in a state of glucose depletion. Most people do not have the willpower to focus on many habits. So when you are in a depleted state, it becomes easy to give up all the habits instead of just the one.

Strategy 2: Take Up a 30-Day Habit-Change Challenge

Take up the challenge to change one habit over a period of thirty days. This is why you need 100 percent commitment. The easy way to do this is via a thirty-day habit challenge. In this challenge, you structure the entire life around the completion of a single specific habit target. You will do other things surely, but a significant amount of your time and willpower will be spent on working toward this target. Sometimes thirty days are not enough. For really challenging habits, such as smoking and drinking, you need more time to make the habit change stick. Do not be afraid of planning for more time. There is nothing wrong in blocking out sixty- to ninety-day period for focusing on this target.

Strategy 3: Set a Starting Date

Set a starting date for the challenge. Soon or next week or eventually will never happen. Just write down the date on which you will start the habit-change challenge. It is significant to take up the target seriously, so having an official countdown will help in keeping you on track. Also, you need to tell your family and friends about the challenge and get their support. Having a start date generates energy and excitement for the challenge and the new change. The aim is to improve your life dramatically so you need to feel energized with the countdown.

Strategy 4: Identifying the Goal

Removing the bad habits from your life is like setting goals. You will not achieve it without having specific goals in mind together with target dates. For example, you can't just say, "I wish to eat healthier." Rather, you need to identify what food you are going to eat, what to avoid, and the day on which these changes will take effect. So a better target will be "From December 1, I will not eat fast food available at places such as McDonald's or KFC. Rather, I will eat home-cooked food that combines vegetables with unrefined carbohydrates and lean protein." See how this goal has a definite deadline and a specific outcome. By December 1, you will know whether it is working out or not. That is the way to set goals for breaking habits.

Strategy 5: Avoiding Cold-Turkey Solutions

All cold-turkey solutions have been tried before. Make a promise that you will not pick the bad habit again and see within a few days you are doing the exact routine you swore you would eliminate forever. Agreed, quitting the cold turkey works sometimes. We are all aware of people who gave up smoking or other vices via a force of will and did not fell off the wagon. However, behind every success story, there are hundreds of people who tried cold-turkey solutions regularly only to experience defeat every time. The main issue with cold-turkey solutions is the overemphasis on perfection. Many people have a negative mind-set. One mistake and it is termed as a failure.

No one is perfect. Having the never-again goals leaves you with no space to wiggle when you are tempted to do the habit you are trying to eliminate. Believe me, we all slip from time to time; therefore, concentrating on perfection cannot be a way for changing a stubborn routine. What is problematic is that the cold turkey can make bad habits go even worse. Many times when people are working with 100 percent perfection goals, they develop a "what the heck" mind-set while they are making a mistake.

As it is, by doing the bad habit, they have already broken the never-again rule. So now they subconsciously decide that since it has already happened once, you might as well repeat. And the result is that the person is more in the grip of the bad habit than ever before.

Strategy 6: Set Some Baseline Metrics

The most successful way of making permanent changes is to concentrate on everyday incremental improvements. The aim is to wean yourself away from this habit by setting goals where you constantly reduce the time or quantity of the bad habit. The first step of the process is to establish baseline metrics. These can vary with the specific habit you are trying to change.

- the number of cigarettes you smoke every day
- the number of times you bite your fingernails
- your current weight
- how many drinks you consume when going out
- the number of calories you burn every day
- amount of time you spend on watching TV
- amount of time spent on surfing the net or on Facebook

Strategy 7: Develop Incremental Goals

As described before, quitting cold turkey is not realistic in the longer run. Rather, focus on incremental goals in which case you slowly move away from the bad habit. For example, let's assume that you smoke twenty cigarettes every day. When you are thinking about changing this bad habit, the ultimate goal is to get clear of the bad practice entirely. But for now, stick to the incremental goals:

- For the first couple of weeks, have fifteen cigarettes instead of twenty.
- For weeks 3 and 4, have ten cigarettes every day.
- For weeks 5 and 6, have five cigarettes.
- For weeks 7 and 8, have three cigarettes.
- Just a single cigarette from ninth week onward.

Of course, your numbers will be different. In addition, there will be times when you will fail in the attempts. The key is in making slow changes to your life. Breaking the bad habit in a methodical way provides your mind and body a chance to destroy the continuous craving.

Phase 2: Understanding the Habit Loop / Forming New Habits

Since you are reading this book, let's assume that you are interested in making a permanent change in your life. In reality, it is not enough to make just the small incremental changes. The best strategy for long-term benefits is to identify the habit loops and understand the underlying motivation behind all the routines. Duhigg talks about habit loops in his book *The Power of Habit*. Habit loops are the activities that bring you from just the cue to a reward.

Understand the actions, and you will take your first step toward making permanent lifestyle changes. The best method for eliminating a bad habit forever is to gradually replace it with healthy habits. This means that instead of focusing on what you are missing, you can follow newer routines that give you the same rewards. When you have scheduled the starting date, you can use the following strategies to reprogram your mind.

Strategy 8: Identifying the Habit Routine

All habits follow the same three-step pattern:

1. **Cue**—a trigger arriving out of a situation based on the rewards you are seeking.
2. **Reward**—the satisfaction you wish for by following the routines.
3. **Routine**—an emotional or physical action you take for obtaining the rewards.

There are always thoughts and actions that occur beforehand and are related to habits. The cue is actually the trigger that creates the craving for getting the reward. Routine is the action necessary for satisfying the impulse. The reward is the satisfaction you get by following the routine or the removal of stress that was created by the cues. The best method to understand the procedure is by going over each component. Let's see how to do that.

Strategy 9: Make a Record of Habit Cues

We are continuously bombarded with triggers to take some actions. Many times, they are external when a sound, smell, or sight develops a craving. On other days, it is an internal sensation that sparks the desire. In order to make permanent changes, you need to fully understand why and when the triggers occur. This can easily be done by recording five bits of information when you feel the requirement to finish a bad habit.

1. **Location:** Note where you are.
2. **Time:** Make a note of the exact time when you feel the urge.
3. **Mood:** Note your emotional state.
4. **People:** Who is around you or with you?
5. **Action:** What are you doing at present? What did you just do?

Repetition is the key to the exercise. Concentrate on recording the five data points in the first few weeks of the new changes in habits. You can do this for a while, and you can notice a number of patterns that provide great insight into bad habits. For example, let's say that you are trying to control your alcohol consumption habit. It might seem like an innocent activity on the surface, but the drinking habit has led to a number of other issues, such as arguments at home, DUI, or decreased productivity at home. What once was a fun activity has become a serious issue now.

In addition to getting help from the others, you will get insights on the habit by tracking the triggers. After recording the data carefully, you will notice that the five patterns stand out:

1. **Location:** At O'Reilly's bar
2. **Time:** 5:00 p.m.
3. **Mood:** Tired and stressed out

4. **People:** With friends Bill, Tom, and Dick
5. **Action:** Watching the baseball game

The goal is to minimize drinking, so after keeping track of the bad habit for some weeks, you realize that the issue occurs at a time when you are stressed out or feel like hanging out. The guys at the time are watching the ball game. By analyzing the triggers, you now realize that the drinking is as a result of the desire to reduce strain and feel stress-free. More significantly, it is an activity you prefer to share with others.

Strategy 10: Work Out Various Rewards

The interesting fact about bad habits is that they often come with a desire for some rewards. Normally, we do them because we wish to be relaxed, energized, happy, and loved. The good part is that you may substitute bad habits and still find positive results. So that is the reason it is important to experiment with different rewards. Prepare a few strategies you can implement when you experience a trigger. The target here is to find positive routines that will give the same feeling you get with bad habits without following negative routines. For example, let's see an example we discussed before—consuming too many drinks. After locating the cues for the first few days, you will realize that drinking habits come from a desire to feel relaxed and a wish to reduce stress. It is a byproduct of the wish to socialize and have fun. Therefore, you may plan various strategies when you have to relax:

- Go for a ten-minute walk around your neighborhood.
- Avoid O'Reilly's bar and cafe.
- Do a different activity with friends rather than drinking.
- Make new connections and build your social network.

Not all the strategies will apply to your situation, but having a strategy is important as you are trying to find a new routine that provides rewards that are similar to bad habits.

Strategy 11: Check What Works

When you follow new routines, take stock of your moods later to see if you still have the desire to do bad habits. If it is still there, then you need to realize that the results of the new routine are not the rewards you are looking for. Let's check the drinking example again.

You found out that exercise and meditation are not decreasing your stress levels. But what did succeed was making new friends with guys who didn't spend the time in a bar. These new friends are the positive people who make you feel relaxed, which ultimately reduces the tense feeling you get before having drinks.

Also, you are aware that one of your buddies Bill (from O'Reilly's bar) loves to go trekking, which is another activity you like. It means you can minimize your drinking and stay connected with your older friends.

When you encounter a bad habit cue, you need to substitute it with newer routines. It will be hard to do in the beginning; however, later you will begin to follow different routines without even thinking about them. Many times, you realize that some people trigger bad habits, which means that when you make a decision, either you spend lesser time with them or you will keep on doing other things that are not good for you. Agreed it is not easy to let go of some people, but many times you must sacrifice relationships that lead to self-destructive loops of habits.

Strategy 12: Devise a Plan to Break the Bad Habit

It will take some weeks of experimentation to find out a perfect replacement for the existing bad habit. But you will definitely find something that works. Here you need to align your activities with this habit instead of to the bad one. The best ways to create lasting changes are to follow step-by-step plans when you experience certain impulses. Get started by picking the common cues from strategy 9 and create a plan for every one of the triggers.

The goal of the exercise is to reprogram your mind to take different actions even when you are feeling the craving to perform the bad habit. For example, once again, let's consider the alcohol habit example. Here are some more strategies to follow:

- When Bill invites me to O'Reilly, I will suggest a trek instead of the session.
- On the basketball Sunday, I will go for activities to be found at meetup.com rather than hitting the bar again.
- At 5:00 p.m. each day, I will take a thirty-minute walk to reduce the stress.

What you are doing here is locating the weak spots and creating a plan for the actions you will take. This is to be the first line of defense against the impulse for the bad habit. Therefore, when the craving comes, you will know exactly what to do.

Strategy 13: Get to Know the Hot-Cold Empathy Gap

There is an old military saying, "All plans are great till the actual first shot is fired." All plans look great on paper, but they very rarely work when you experience great temptations. You may be able to do it well for some time, but it is difficult to stick to new routines when your life has stress and cues leading to them. And it is difficult to remember while making plans what it is like to feel that craving that affects you psychologically and physically.

You may believe that you will not cave in, but it is hard to do when you are under stress, tired, or just want to do the one thing you are trying to stop. Once this happens, it is significant to remember what one George Lowenstein mentioned in one of his researches. Basically, he derived that people suffer from something called hot-cold empathy gap when they are making plans for dealing with temptations.

Once it comes to hot-cold empathy gap, most people fail to judge how they will feel in the hot state once there is a strong desire for a bad habit. In other words, no matter how much you plan it is difficult to understand what it is like to actually experience strong cravings. The point being, although it is significant to plan, you will need strategies while dealing with slipups. Remember, mistakes are mistakes, and caving in will not make you weak. Rather, accept the fact that you will succumb occasionally to some desire, and it is a natural process to making permanent habit changes. Mistakes do happen, and failing is not the end as long as you begin again, only a bit wiser.

Strategy 14: Use of Habit Reminders for Staying on Course

Habit reminder is a fantastic way to keep following new routines. They can be written on a piece of paper that you keep all the time with you, or they may be a part of an alert that pops up on the cell phone. Although these reminders may sound silly, they are great methods for keeping the habit change process at the forefront of your mind.

Phase 3: Build Support Systems to Aid You in Breaking Bad Habits

Making a commitment to changing yourself is only half the battle. Actually, you cannot make lasting changes on your own. Rather, it is significant to build support systems of people that will aid you in following through with the target. People are capable of either making or breaking your efforts. By adding them to your habit change plans, you can get help when you are feeling weak or tempted. Here are some strategies for creating great support systems to aid you to change a bad habit.

Strategy 15: Maintain a Journal for Accountability

Keep track of your everyday attempts at changing your habits, including the statistics and metrics. The more info you include, the easier it is to understand what affects your impulses or moods. Although this depends on the habits, here are some things you may include in your accountability journal:

- the number of times you repeated the bad habit
- total calories consumed, burned, and broken down to individual food
- amount of time spent on doing the bad habit
- the current weight and BMI (body mass index)
- emotions, feelings, and impulses
- challenges you are experiencing currently

For example, let's say you wish to quit smoking. Each day you have to set a limit for the maximum number of cigarettes you will smoke. Then note down the actual number of cigarettes you smoked. Add to this record all the feelings and impulses that led to the activity. The main thing about the accountability journal is providing 100 percent disclosure. You must write down all the details even if you actually fail in your attempt to achieve the goal.

Strategy 16: Make Public Declarations

The social networks have become major parts of our daily existence. One of the great methods for harnessing the friendship is requesting support for the habit change target.

No one wishes to look bad. Post the updates about the habit change attempts on your social networks and see that you will get encouragement from your online friends. It could be a Facebook post or just a tweet. You can also use mobile apps for this, such as coach.me, which updates your account automatically with progress reports. Do not underestimate the capabilities of social approvals. Just by knowing that you will be accountable for the habits alone will keep you focused on the change.

Strategy 17: Find One Accountability Partner

There is no need to do this alone. Rather, you must communicate regularly with someone who shares a similar desire to make lasting habit changes. Meet or even just talk to this person every week a few times and share your experiences. You may take all this a step further and create a new routine together, such as walking ten thousand steps together. Another idea is to find a sponsor that can help you in getting through the moments of weakness. Just call this person when you are feeling susceptible, and they will help you get past the temptation. It is not required that the accountability partner has to live close by. It is easy to meet folks on media and Facebook groups. You can find some people who share the common wish to grow good habits. All you need to do is install Skype or a similar tool, and you can talk for five minutes or so at a time every week.

Strategy 18: Ignore the Negative People (Naysayers)

It is sad, but there will be people who consciously or subconsciously will try to sabotage your efforts at self-improvement. These could be close friends, random strangers, or even close family members. These words can be like poison as they flood your attention with self-limiting opinions. If you listen to their advice, it will be at your own peril. You are doomed the instant you start trusting them as it is a first and sure step toward letdown. Having a plan for these naysayers is as significant as knowing what to do when tempted with impulses. You must know what to do and what to say when a person says something that puts doubts in your mind about the habit change. It is strongly recommended that you find a way to ignore the comments or instantly rebuff the remarks.

Strategy 19: Avoid the Trigger Locations

People are not the only cues toward a bad habit. Many times a location can raise an impulse to follow specific routines. At the time when you are attempting to change a routine, you will need to avoid places that cause negative bad loops. For example, a lot of people smoke when they are drinking. Therefore, when you are looking to break a smoking habit, it is good to avoid the bar scene altogether. Yes, it may mean ditching your friends for a while; however, the strategy will help you minimize the opportunities where you will feel like lighting up.

Strategy 20: Get Professional Help

Let's be honest about this. There are some habits that need a greater level of expertise that goes beyond just reading a piece of content on the internet. Many times, you will have to seek professional help or attend meetings to get rid of strong addictions. There are several bad habits that require professional help, such as drug addiction, alcoholism, chain-smoking, binge eating, and eating disorders. It is not possible to tell here where the line lies in your case, but it is possible that you are at a point where you need a hand from a pro. Here are some ways to implement the strategy:

- Talk to a psychiatrist or psychologist.
- Join groups such as AA (Alcoholics Anonymous) or NA (Narcotics Anonymous).
- Join some local weight-loss group that emphasizes permanent lifestyle changes rather than fad diets.
- Talk to your doctor about various non-addictive solutions to negate the cravings.

Do not be afraid to get aid from people. You may have some strong addiction that is not possible to get rid of with simple checklists. The possibility is, if you think you have a real issue at hand, then it is better to get assistance that is needed.

Phase 4: Overcoming the Challenges That Are Essential in Breaking Bad Habits

Do you still remember our description about hot-cold empathy gap? It is something you will encounter when trying to do major habit-change challenges. The key lies in following some specific strategies to overcome the empathy gap. Just implement the following, and you will be able to fight the moments of weakness or temptations.

Strategy 21: Lead a Healthy Lifestyle

As mentioned before, self-image depletion can lead to your willpower getting to a weakened state. When you are always hungry, tired, depressed, or stressed, you will raise the chances of succumbing to temptations. An easy way to contest ego diminution is to lead a healthy lifestyle. As this problem is caused largely to low glucose levels, you may fight the temptations by doing the following:

- getting a full night sleep and feel energized in the morning
- staying hydrated by drinking at least eight cups of water each day
- eating balanced food each day, including vegetables, fruits, lean protein, and good carbohydrates
- exercising to maintain optimum weight and reduce stress
- keeping healthy snacks with you for the times when you will feel hungry

Never underestimate the power of mind-body connection. When you are leading a balanced and healthy life, breaking the bad habits becomes that much easier.

Strategy 22: Stay Positive

Everybody has temptations as a result of bad habits. It is a natural part of the procedure, so do not allow these feelings to suppress you. The trick lies in knowing what to do when you are experiencing an impulse. The moment you receive a pang for a bad habit, keep firm to your commitment to stick with the new plans. You may even recite an easy mantra for this whenever you get the moment of weakness. It could easily be just a silly phrase you repeat regularly, such as "Alcohol-free within six months." Repeat it over and over when you feel the urge to take a drink.

Strategy 23: Stay Away from "What the Hell" Attitude

As discussed before, it is easy to slip up with your targets. What you do not afford to do is develop a "what the hell" mind-set. In this case, you have basically given up and have marched on to a binge as you have already failed for that particular day. Although it is okay to mess up from time to time, what you cannot do is get off the deep end when you have succumbed to temptation. Agreed tomorrow is another day; however, it cannot be used as an excuse to get carried away with the bad habits.

For example, your target is to have less than ten cigarettes daily, and you slipped up on one day and ended up smoking twelve cigarettes. What you must not do is follow the inclination that says, "What the hell, as I have already smoked twelve, I might as well finish the rest of the day by lighting up some more whenever I feel like." The "what the hell" attitude is a potent threat to the habit-change process. When you goof up, just accept the failure and concentrate on minimizing the damage. Significantly, do not use it as an excuse to do more bad things, such as smoking additional cigarettes.

Strategy 24: Forgive Yourselves for Small Failures

One of the major reasons why people end up giving up habit change is because they have no idea what to do when they have fallen off the wagon. Surely, they will follow the goals strictly for a few weeks, but they do not know what to do in case they slip up. What happens many times is that they use a mistake as an excuse to give up. At a dangerous risk of sounding like a strange psychologist, what is needed here is forgiving yourself. Everybody makes mistakes, but beating yourself over the slipups is not good for the long-term goals.

Although it is significant to be strict about removing bad habits, you must avoid developing negative thoughts in your head. Well, a mistake is a mistake, and it doesn't mean you are weak or do not have willpower. It means you are human, just like the rest of us.

Strategy 25: Reward Yourself

Changing bad habits and developing good ones can turn out to be a grueling experience. It is up to you to make it fun by setting rewards for achieving specific milestones. The important thing here is not to have an incentive that is directly bad for the habit-changing exercise you are performing. For example, whenever you meet your weight-loss goal for the week, you may treat yourself to a film or have a little shopping spree. However, you need to avoid the all-you-can-eat buffets, such as Golden Corral.

Set some rewards for achieving the habit-change target. Have an incentive for day 1, first week, second week, first month, third month, sixth month, and one-year milestones. The more targets you have, the more focused you stay on the habit-change exercise.

Strategy 26: Review Your Plans Daily

Getting rid of the bad habit is similar to any other long-term goal. Fundamentally, you require daily commitments and reminders for sticking to the plans. One of the strategies is to turn the habit-change process into a target you will review every single day. For example, I have a morning habit where I go over all the goals I have set and reaffirm my commitment to make changes in my life.

Strategy 27: Work Day by Day

Do not worry about what will happen tomorrow or after one year. Rather, focus on the next cue or trigger. Set a plan for what you will do today, and worry about the tomorrow when it arrives. Changing a habit is similar to running a marathon. You will go mad if you think about running 26.2 miles. However, it is easier to complete if you stay focused on running the next mile. Keep concentrating on what you need to do right now and try to ignore what will happen later in the future.

Having this mind-set will help you in making slow but incremental changes. In the beginning, you may notice a shift in the habits. But when there is a longer timeline involved, you will be able to incorporate changes in your lifestyle and your routines. You used to fall for the bad habits in the past, but now you can resist the urge.

Conclusion (Breaking Bad Habits)

Breaking bad habits is an involvement topic, so it has taken everyone a while to get there. So let us recap what we have learned so far. Breaking bad habits is an ongoing process that doesn't happen overnight. We have discussed twenty-seven strategies in this chapter that will definitely assist you in making lasting changes. However, at the end of the day, it is significant to remember that these are only tips. Actual results come when you take action. Read the book and go step-by-step through all ideas. Begin by selecting a single bad habit and make aggressive attempts to eliminate the habit totally.

You might try your best and yet find that you are sabotaging your efforts at making habit changes. In case you are consistently behaving in ways that will make you unhealthy or unhappy, you might be psychologically attached to the habits. In order to find out more about the psychological attachments, read on. If you have any specific problem, there are many books available on the internet.

You need to remember that changing bad habits needs daily commitment. You need to work hard and stay focused. However, do not agonize over failures. It is important to keep at it and, in the process, learn from all the triggers or impulses. You will see yourself kicking away the bad habits in no time.

Chapter 8: Eating, Fitness, Health, and Lifestyle Habits

We keep hearing that having healthy habits, such as staying active, eating healthy, and staying on top of our health screening, is very important. However, have you actually thought about why the changes are so significant and how they work together? Healthy habits are those including anything that you do to benefit your mental, physical, or emotional well-being. These habits, when put together, will help in creating a framework for healthy living. In case you are not familiar with a healthy lifestyle, the habits are tough to develop as you need to alter your mind-set a little bit and even alter your everyday schedule.

But if you are really ready to be committed to improving your health, you can start having healthy habits to benefit you in the longer run. It doesn't matter how old you are or how terrible your older habits were; you can improve them and move forward to create a better lifestyle for you. It's significant to note that healthy habits are created in stages. What is an unhealthy habit for a person may be a healthy habit for another.

For example, let's say that you have an unhealthy habit of having two big bowls of ice cream every night before you go to sleep. Cutting the amount of ice cream down to one bowl or even half a bowl is progress in your case toward healthy habits of pushing done the unhealthy food consumption. But for somebody who doesn't eat any ice cream at night, it is not healthy progress. Stay where you are and then make progress toward healthy habits that are good for you.

In case you have developed a health condition, it is not healthy to start training for a long-distance race, such as a marathon. Do not try to emulate experienced long-distance runners out of the blue. However, it might be a good idea to start going for everyday walks in order to be more active. In this list of healthy habits, you can learn about eating well, working out, and having an overall healthy life. There are things that apply to some and not to others, but habits are a good starting point for people who might be looking to improve themselves.

Physical Fitness

Having physical activity will benefit both your mind and body. It also aids in keeping your weight in control and fight off the chronic diseases. It reduces stress, improves the mood, and provides a sense of accomplishment to you. Having physical exercise does not mean long hours at the gym; rather, there are several ways in which you can make small adjustments throughout the day and make your life less sedentary by making your body move.

You may also involve your family and friends in the activity so that you can have some time for interacting with people you love and also benefitting the body. There are many kinds of physical activities that can be added to your daily routine, but it is significant to find out the one that you enjoy doing, and then stick to it.

1. Do the housework.
2. Take a thirty-minute early morning walk.
3. Implement a two-minute-per-hour walking habit while working at desks.
4. Remember to take the stairs rather than using elevators wherever possible.
5. Try to walk as much as possible.
6. Use a treadmill desk.
7. Use height-adjustable desks.
8. Target ten thousand steps every day. You can use a step-tracking device or app for this.
9. Enjoy a dance break.
10. Take to hiking more often.
11. Yoga and meditation are good.
12. Go for rock climbing.
13. Enjoy geocaching.
14. Workout while commercials are shown during TV programs.

15. Do the desk exercises.

Forgiveness

Although forgiveness might seem like an antiquated notion to the quick-to-react and rushed society, there are several health benefits in it even in modern society. Once you are able to let go of something consciously even without an apology, your anger levels go down along with stress and tension. The physical burden involved in being hurt takes a heavy toll on the body. Therefore, being able to release negative feelings and replacing them with positive ones is a good habit.

By choosing not to forgive someone, you are increasing your anger, and it contributes toward a lack of control. Holding a grudge leads to muscular tension, increased heart rate, and high blood pressure. It is all harmful to your health. If you are able to forgive someone, it improves your sleeping pattern. You will stop spending time in bed ruminating over things that happened in the past or planning your retaliation. If you could meditate and completely forgive people, you will be able to focus more on yourself and your own well-being.

And most importantly, if you are able to forgive, it increases the strength of your relationship with your family and friends. You need to avoid the deep-rooted strains in your close relationships as it is an important part of being connected to the people around you. Try to lead a life in harmony with people that cross your path as keeping good relations is a key part of leading a healthy lifestyle.

1. Do not sleep in anger.
2. Concentrate on understanding yourself rather than blaming others.
3. Live in the present. Don't get stuck over the past.
4. Do things for yourselves and for your own peace of mind.
5. Remember those occasions when you were forgiven for your mistakes.
6. Remember those friends when they were small.

7. Remember to know why you love certain people.
8. Always remember that it is better to be kind rather than to be right.
9. Just observe; do not judge people.
10. Take ownership of your own shortcomings.
11. Acknowledge that you have grown with experience.

Healthy Eating with Portion-Size Control

Many times, it is not "what" you are eating but "how much" you are consuming. For instance, avocados are very healthy and have much to offer in terms of healthy fats and nutrients. But they are very thick in calories, and eating three of the avocados in a single day is not very healthy. You need to eat till you are physically satisfied, and after that, stop. In case you still feel hungry, wait for twenty minutes and drink a glass of water. After that, consider if you still need any more helpings.

Remember to start eating in smaller plates as it makes you feel as if the plate is full just before your dinner. You will be shocked to know the quantity of food that amounts to a single serving. Always keep in mind that eating is not a pastime, and it is not something you do when stressed out or bored. Ensure that you eat mindfully while it is time to do so. You need to sit down and eat properly, being focused on just the food.

Mindless eating while watching the TV or making visits to the fridge when you had a bad day or both are bad habits that lead to further health issues in the future. Remember, overindulgence into anything, even something as clear and pure as water, can be intoxicating.

1. Do not eat when you are feeling stressed.
2. Make use of portion control containers for storing your meal.
3. Use portion control plates while eating at home.
4. Listen to the hunger pangs.
5. Drink a lot of water and other healthy fluids.
6. Maintain a journal or a diary.
7. Prepare and have healthy smoothies.
8. Learn to read the nutrition labels.
9. Keep away from the candy bars and other such stuff.

10. Plan your meals for the week.
11. Make single serving snack packs.
12. Avoid distractions while having the meal.
13. Consume daily probiotics.
14. Stick to the list of groceries.
15. Use turmeric supplements.
16. Take small bites while eating and eat slowly.
17. Chew the food at least seven to eight times before swallowing it.
18. Drink before being thirsty.

Preventive Health Care

People generally go to a doctor when they are not feeling well or when there are some unknown symptoms creeping up. From here on, the doctor works with the patient to diagnose and treat the problem with the intention to make it go away. But what if there is no health problem in the first place? For example, when you have noticed a small mark of your skin, which apparently popped up from nowhere, and you are not aware of what it is, it could be a symptom of skin cancer, which could spread quickly through the body. Rather, be proactive and go to a dermatologist periodically to get checkups done so that they can check your skin for any defects that may be suspicious.

It is vital to be sensitive about your health regardless of whether you are actually ill or not. Doctors can give advice on preventive measures for sicknesses that run in the family or even catch a problem early before it is too late. Catching the problem early is the key. Therefore, ensure that you pay attention to health no matter how you are feeling at that moment.

1. physical examination every year
2. thyroid tests for women
3. bone mineral density test for women
4. mammogram for women
5. glucose test
6. colonoscopy
7. eye examination
8. hearing test
9. dental cleaning and examination
10. abdominal aortic aneurysm screening for men
11. cholesterol screening
12. blood pressure screening
13. prostrate checking for men

14. screening for lung cancer
15. self-examination of testicles for men
16. Pap testing and HPV testing for women
17. chlamydia testing for women
18. gonorrhea testing for women
19. testing for HIV and other sexually transmitted diseases
20. skin testing
21. flu vaccination
22. hepatitis A vaccination
23. hepatitis B vaccination
24. herpes zoster vaccination
25. HPV (human papillomavirus) vaccination
26. MMR (measles, mumps, and rubella)
27. meningitis
28. pneumonia vaccination
29. tetanus, diphtheria, and pertussis
30. chickenpox

Suggested Timelines for Routine Health Screenings

For Men

- **Physical exam**—every two to three years for those eighteen and over.
- **Colonoscopy**—within seven to ten years for those fifty and over.
- **Eye exam**—once before the age of thirty, as recommended by a doctor when you are past the age of forty, and every one to two years after age sixty-five.
- **Hearing test**—once every ten years for people aged eighteen to fifty, once every three years for men aged fifty-one and over.
- **Dental cleaning**—twice every year for men over the age of eighteen.
- **Blood pressure screening**—every two years after the age is past eighteen.
- **Cholesterol screening**—every five years after you reach the age thirty-five.
- **Prostate screening**—starting at the age fifty.
- **Skin exam**—yearly, beginning from the age of eighteen.

For Women

- **Physical exam**—annually.
- **Bone mineral density test**—start at the age of sixty-five.
- **Mammogram**—every one to two years beginning at forty.
- **Clinical breast exam**—every three years for women who are between the ages of twenty and forty years.
- **Colonoscopy**—every seven to ten years for the women fifty and over.
- **Fasting plasma glucose test**—every three years beginning at the age forty-five.
- **Eye exam**—once before the age of thirty, as recommended by doctors after age forty, every one to two years after age sixty-five.
- **Dental cleaning**—twice annually for women over eighteen.
- **Blood pressure screening**—every two years starting at the age of eighteen.
- **Cholesterol screening**—every five years starting at the age of thirty-five.
- **Pap test**—every three years for women aged between twenty-one and twenty-nine, every five years for women between thirty and sixty-five (testing might be discontinued at age sixty-five in case there is no previous occurrence of a problem).
- **Skin exam**—annually after the age of eighteen.

Get Sufficient Sleep for healthy living

Sleep has an important role to play in maintaining the general well-being and a healthy lifestyle. It is important to get sufficient dark sleep in the nights as it protects your physical and mental health, along with your overall quality of life and safety as well. How you will feel when you are awake depends largely on the quality of sleep you got earlier at night. When you are sleeping, the body goes on a recovery path and then replenishes itself to support healthy functioning of your brain and optimizing your physical health. It also plays a vital role in the development and growth of children.

Sleep deficiencies occur both quickly and over a period. In case you are not getting enough sleep on a regular basis, you are at the risk of chronic health issues. You may experience troubled thinking during the days, have bad days at the office, have delayed reactions, have issues developing new relationships, and experience learning problems.

You must provide your body a chance to restore from a day of expenditure of energy and prepare for the next day where you are going to need more energy. If you fail to do so, you will definitely suffer. To aid this objective, consider the following:

1. Avoid coffee and similar beverages in the afternoons.
2. Do not take heavy meals at the time when you are getting ready to go to bed.
3. Always keep the pets away from the bed.
4. Have a consistent sleeping schedule.
5. Never drink too much fluid just before bedtime.
6. Stop smoking.
7. If you have an air conditioner, set the temperature to 60–70°F.
8. Turn off all the electronics one hour before bedtime.
9. Wear socks.
10. Do meditation.

11. Visualize happy thoughts.
12. Keep a log of the amount of sleep and quality of sleep you are getting.
13. Have a sleep routine with a wind-down.
14. Learn to get back to sleep.
15. Ensure that your room is quiet and dark.
16. Use the necessary oil diffusers with the right essential oils for getting sleep.

Go for Something New Such as a Healthy Lifestyle

Everybody gets into a typical routine in which they are doing the same things pretty much all day, but there are many methods for mixing up the schedule a tad so that you may try new things. Changing a boring routine helps in challenging yourself and helps in learning new things. In case you were hesitant in the beginning, you may end up enjoying the new activities or the new people you will meet. Trying new things leads to raised confidence and a high level of self-esteem when you are decreasing the loneliness and boredom. This is also useful in developing personal growth, increasing longevity, and improving your health.

1. Learn new languages.
2. Watch foreign language films having subtitles.
3. Go to a new restaurant for food. Allow the waiter to decide your meal.
4. Travel to a new place you have not visited before.
5. Sign for a new class that is related to your work.
6. Try your hand at a new sport.
7. Cook an easy dinner you haven't tried before.
8. Go to work on a different route or use a different mode of transport.
9. Go on a road trip.
10. Make changes in your appearance and sport a new look.
11. Listen to different kind of music than you are used to.
12. Read books from authors you have never heard of.
13. Try a new kind of exercise.
14. Watch a new musical or a play.
15. Watch drag shows.
16. Ban the internet for one week from your life.
17. Spend the weekend without expenditure.

Improve Fitness by Working on Strength and Flexibility

Everyone has a tendency to lose strength and decrease in size naturally with age. They also become less supple and get stiffer. Your range of movement gets affected due to these changes, and it affects the joints more and causes you to lose elasticity. This finally leads to tight muscles. One of the most important reasons that cause muscles to weaken and lose flexibility is lack of activity. You must do the strength- and flexibility-building exercises. Loss of flexibility might lead to permanent damage to your posture, and it will result in a loss of healthy muscles. Therefore, it is imperative that you maintain great muscle flexibility, which can be a significant part of your overall fitness.

Having these flexible muscles helps in reducing the soreness in the body and helps improve the posture. Stretching will also improve the overall muscular balance with the realignment of tissue in the body that decreases the efforts required to keep the balance. By having strong muscles and flexibility, you are decreasing the risk of injuries and allowing yourself a larger range of movement.

Lastly, practicing the healthy habits increases the nutrients and blood that are delivered to the tissues inside your body. The reason is that when you stretch, you raise the temperature of the tissues, and as a result, there is a rise in blood circulation and transport of nutrients. Here are some easy exercises:

1. crunches
2. push-ups
3. curl to press
4. lying march
5. fly to tris
6. ball squat
7. tripod row

8. dips
9. arm across the chest
10. shoulder and chest
11. triceps stretch
12. adductor stretch
13. glute stretch
14. single leg hamstring
15. standing quadriceps

Laughter for a Healthy Living

Many researchers think that laughter, indeed, is the best medicine as it helps you feel good and reduces stress. Laughter plays an important role in having a positive attitude and being open to the possibility of letting loose. Also, having a great sense of humor also goes a long way in creating relationships with people. It also helps in forming strong bonds.

Different researches have concluded that when people are laughing, their brains go through the similar changes as that when they are meditating explicitly. It makes people feel refreshed and ready to take on the world. You can also encounter problems within a day that are better handled in a positive state of mind. Although the therapeutic value of laughter is still under study, so far it has only shown positive effects.

1. Learn about the therapeutic advantages of laughter.
2. Make a commitment toward laughing more.
3. Watch the silly movies and TV shows.
4. Go to a yoga laughter club.
5. Consider joining a laughter based exercise program.
6. Engage in self-initiated and voluntary laughter.
7. Spare some time to watch the funny videos available on the internet.
8. Spend even more time with the pets.
9. Read newspaper comics and funny books.
10. Watch the programs of your favorite comedian.
11. Watch some stand-up comedy shows available live on YouTube.
12. Hear out the funny podcasts.
13. Meet old friends and reminisce with them.
14. Visit amusement parks.

15. Watch your old photos and laugh.

Spending Time with Family and Friends

Humans are social animals and are not meant to live alone. We come to this world with the mother and possibly other immediate family members around. Through the different stages in our lives, we depend on other people to provide assistance and help for accomplishing various things. For doing almost anything, you must have cooperation from other people. We have evolved in such a manner that we must cooperate to survive. Having a family and friends whom you are able to rely on, turn to, and mix with will provide you an additional sense of belonging. It allows you to relate with others who share the same values as you do and also the same beliefs.

The most significant part of self-care is to turn it into a priority and move on to develop and maintain good relationships. Many times, it takes special efforts to do so due to our busy lifestyle. But keeping up with our old loved ones and friends is a very healthy habit to have.

1. Always have dinner with your family together on the table.
2. Keep the time reserved for a weekly night with the family.
3. Always take time for yearly vacations with the family.
4. Do chores, exercise, and play with the family.
5. Read bedtime stories to the kids, and share interesting books with the elders.
6. Keep family photo albums, and in fact, allow the albums to grow.
7. Make acquaintance with your child's friends.
8. Help the children with their homework.
9. Go on camping trips together.
10. Take the children to school.
11. Leave the family encouraging or love notes.
12. Work with the family or friends on the common goals. Be an accountability partner for each other.

13. Host sleepover nights.
14. Plan reading dates with friends.
15. Help friends with chores.
16. Meet friends for lunch at least once monthly.

Take Care of the Negative Addictive Behaviors

When you say the word *addictive*, the only thing that emerges in front of everyone is alcohol/drugs/tobacco addiction, but there are other things, such as behaviors that are equally addictive and damaging. They may be healthy when moderated but can end up being addictions. These things can be anything from coffee, food, internet use, or gambling. They are all addictive to some people. There are some levels that are considered as safe for these kinds of behaviors. We must recognize them to address our habits accordingly. We must know when something is being done in excess. Remember to consider your personality while doing this. Researches have indicated that there is a connection between compulsive behavior, impulsiveness, and addiction. You need to be able to reflect yourself to judge if you have any repetitive bad behavior that is without rational motivation.

A fully grown addiction happens when you are incapable of stopping a harmful behavior pattern even when you realize that it has negative consequences. When you identify a problem, it is important that you act to address it.

1. Begin by admitting that there is a problem.
2. Visualize the consequences of addictive behavior.
3. Try to assess how bad the thing has become.
4. Know your personality and consider it carefully.
5. Find out the reason behind the behavior.
6. Discover the habit loop and identify the triggers. Learn about breaking bad habits. You can find the guidance in the chapters above.
7. Try to create and engage in a new routine that is different to the other one and disrupts the addictive behavior pattern.
8. Keep the accountability journal, such as freedom journal.

9. Reward yourself for achieving the set goals.

10. In case you feel as if you are in need of professional help, consider consulting a therapist.

Quieten Down Your Mind

You can take some time of the day away from everything to quieten your mind and meditate. It is a great method to reduce stress. It will help you to connect the body with the mind and release any tensions that may have built up from things that are happening in your professional or personal life. It will also provide a chance to reflect on everything going on in your life and deal with or accept the problems that have kept you from being successful at achieving your goals. The mind needs rest throughout the day. Only then can it get ready to perform the next task or the new ones coming your way.

1. Practice breathing exercises in the morning.
2. Prepare if-then plans for times when monkey mind starts taking its toll on you.
3. Perform regular meditation in the mornings.
4. Practice shower meditation.
5. Observe your own thoughts.
6. Practice qigong.
7. Practice pranayama.
8. Write the morning pages or keep a journal.
9. Create a coffee or tea ritual.
10. Practice yoga.
11. Recite positive affirmations or mantras.
12. Build concentration.
13. Practice careful eating.
14. Take digital breaks regularly.
15. Take a musical break.
16. Reduce distractions.

Be Grateful

Remind yourself to be grateful for living every day. It will keep your spirits up and fend off all the lingering depressions. Concentrate on the positive aspects of your life instead of the negative ones and keep in mind your strengths when you are starting every day. Always make it a specific point to be thankful for everything you have in life. It is beneficial to your overall well-being and happiness. Many times, we forget small things, taking them for granted each day. We will not know what to do without them.

1. Maintain a gratitude journal.
2. Give someone a compliment at least one every day.
3. Say thanks.
4. Say grace before the dinner.
5. Every morning, think of three things you must be grateful for.
6. Smile often.
7. Volunteer to do work for causes or organizations you believe in.
8. Write thank-you notes to friends, relatives, or new acquaintances for being a part of your life.
9. Make gratitude collages.
10. Appreciate nature.
11. Listen attentively when someone is talking.
12. Write and send thank-you notes.
13. Look for the helpers.
14. Be thankful when you have learned something new.
15. Reward efforts.

When you are practicing healthy habits, you raise your chances of living a healthier and longer life. Even when you are starting small, you may significantly decrease your chances of development of chronic diseases or dying prematurely. You are far better off than those who live only on unhealthy habits.

It is understandable that bad habits are difficult to break; however, when you are able to get into a routine of practicing good habits, you will not regret the decision to make efforts. As the changes in behavior do not occur overnight, it is significant to be patient and take smaller steps each day at a time. Be considerate, and share the list of healthy habits with family and friends.

Let's hope you found this extensive list of good habits useful. Also, do not be daunted by the sheer number of things you are required to do to live a healthy lifestyle. It is a lot; however, it is not expected that everything must be 100 percent all the time. In case you recognize the significance of healthy habits and do your best to improve incrementally, you will be leagues ahead of those who have no idea about the benefits of healthy living.

Chapter 9: Habit Stacking for Classrooms

Let's see some smart ways of boosting the learning experience by using habit stacking. When we take a look at what the research concludes about getting better at something, there are two pieces of evidence that stand out. First, there must be clarity on what our target is and where we wish to go or what you wish to become. Secondly, it is a deliberate practice combined with feedback loops that increase the myelin in the brain and, in turn, helps in improving the growth and performance.

In this chapter, we will see about the process that is often missed while looking at the success of a student in a classroom. We keep talking about goals, growth, and instruction practice; and we miss the key elements of going from "Define a goal" to "Achieve a goal" with the students. It is about building better learning habits.

We keep talking about strategies but keep forgetting that our habits as a teacher and a leader influence the habits of the students. Students become better at writing only through deliberate practice and feedback on the practice. However, in case the students did not have the habit of writing each day, it is very difficult to improve the practice and reach their writing targets. This is where habit stacking becomes necessary in the classrooms.

S. J. Scott says in his book *Habit Stacking: 97 Small Changes*:

> It's been said that the average person's short-term memory can only retain seven chunks of information. So the theory behind cognitive load is that since you can only retain a small amount of information, you have to rely on long-term memory, habits and established processes to do basically everything in life.

You can trace every success (or failure) in your life back to a habit. What you do on a daily basis largely determines what you'll achieve in life. Habits create routine and let's face it—most of us run our lives by some sort of routine. We get up in the morning and follow a preset pattern: Take a shower, brush our teeth, get dressed, make breakfast, drive to work, do the work and then go home. Some of us choose to follow self-improvement habits: Set goals, read inspirational books, work on important projects and ignore wasteful distractions. Others choose self-destructive habits: Do the bare minimum, dull creativity through low-quality entertainment, eat junk food and blame others for their failures in life.

Although all that is true, it is very difficult to try to start a new habit. Just think about the number of people deciding to start working out, going to a gym, and eating properly on the New Year resolution list. Many people try to build the daily exercise habit several times in their life span only to fail several times. However, what is fascinating is what you did differently when you found success.

Scott has provided alternative practice to building habits in the book on habit stacking:

We all know it's not easy to add dozens of new habits to your day. But what you might not realize is it's fairly easy to build a single new routine. The essence of habit stacking is to take a series of small changes (like eating a piece of fruit or sending a loving text message to your significant other) and build a ritual that you follow on a daily basis. Habit stacking works because you eliminate the stress of trying to change too many things at once. Your goal is to simply focus on a single routine that only takes about 15 to 30 minutes to complete. Within this routine is a series of actions (or small changes). All you have to do is to create a checklist and follow it every single day. That's the essence of habit stacking.

Habit stacking can be utilized in the classrooms and schools in a range of ways. You can see how a daily routine coupled with a morning meeting can have the teachers of kindergarten ready every day. It can be noticed how a strong and daily anticipatory set sets up the students for meaningful learning. You can observe teachers with collaboration and communication norms make students understand what kind of conversations were relevant to learning. All these examples can be traced back to the habits that were developed in classrooms. And every habit can build better practices that are connected to the learning goals.

Building Good Habits for Teachers and Students

Let's see how teachers can build good habits as educators and foster the use of habit stacking in the classrooms. Here are some habits that can be used right now with students:

1. Conversations at the desk or door: Talk to the students about what is going on in their personal lives, and as a result, they will start coming to you for guidance and help and will provide critical feedback. The short but useful conversations spark up the social and human aspects of learning, which is a significant piece of the education puzzle. However, the important thing is to be able to do this to all your students.

2. The entrance work / bell ringer / do now: When you were in college, you must have heard about an "anticipatory set," but who cares about the name? If you travel around the country in educational institutes, you will hear about "do now," "entrance work," "take 5," "bell ringer," and the list goes on and on. You need to think about your favorite TV shows. When you watch it the next time, notice how the initial five minutes of the show are full of action and are able to catch your attention immediately. This is what needs to happen in the classroom as well. Get them to think.

3. Assess the education process: Students are like the rest of us, and they act that way. They will only focus on what is going to be measured or graded and praised. It's your job to make the learning process as important as the actual final product, which could be the project, exam, test, etc. You will see your students blossom this way.

4. Write something each day: Everyone becomes a better reader by writing each day, and you become a better writer by reading every day. Get yourselves along with your students into a writing habit and work on it every day. Make the process enjoyable by using platforms such as Write About, which has terrific visual writing prompts to spark off the student's imagination.

5. Have a transaction with different texts every day: It doesn't matter at what grade you are teaching or the subject you are preaching; students must have a daily habit of going through different texts. Note that all students have to go through different subjects in their average day at school. This daily practice allows the students to make a connection, go deep with analysis, and find out what they really enjoy in reading.

6. Identify and define problems: It is not possible for us to separate the everyday learning from problem-based learning in our classrooms. Try to make each day a problem-solving day. In order to do this, the first step will be to define the problem and then empathize with the issue. Once the students get in the habit of defining a problem to its core, they will also look for solutions that will have the greatest impact.

7. Work for solutions collaboratively: There has to be a reason for collaborative work. Having students in groups and getting them to fill out worksheets is not collaborative work. Rather, concentrate on the habits to solve problems you have defined earlier in group kind of settings. This places everybody on the same team on the same target.

8. Debates: Get your students geared up. John Spencer was the person responsible for having the idea of a daily debate. It is great to have debates in the classroom. Set the rules for the event, talk about what will make a strong argument, and get students to voice their opinions on topics they are interested in. This will ensure that when it is time to write that paper or give the speech, your pupils will be in the habit to make their case stand out.

9. Make/play/tinker/create: Although it might sound an obvious thing to do to get students to make every day, it is difficult to do without having it as a priority. There are far too many scripted curriculums and programs out there that do not allow any space for

"tinker time," and finally, when the students find the opportunity, they prefer to have a worksheet filled out. It is sad, so do make it daily, and you will find students wanting to carry the making back home.

10. Reflecting: Everybody needs to reflect a little more. It is one of the major learning tools to assess yourself and reflect on what you have learned, done, and must do. Get the students to reflect many times daily but keep it short initially. Taking a moment off will revitalize the minds and develop a daily habit of thinking about the thinking. If it is too much, start small. Try just a few things in the classroom and then begin stacking the

habits you have mastered. The daily practices will be one of them. Remember these can be blended in several shapes, ways, or forms; however, the key is to perform the activity daily and then make it stick.

Chapter 10: Relationship Habit Stacking

You need to develop ten minutes of daily routine for growing your social network. Here is how. You will not get very far in your life without having the right people around you. As much as we keep telling ourselves that the achievements we will reach are and will be as a result of hard work, many times being in the right place with the right people is the catalyst that will launch you in a new phase of life, business, or career.

All business owners need good, strong clients, mentors, and employees. Athletes need good coaches along with teammates. In any line, there is always a need to grow and foster relationships with the most significant people. It is of paramount importance as your network is your best asset. The more efficient you are in networking, the truer this statement is. There is a reason behind having a war room full of talented and innovative people by all the successful startups in Silicon Valley. They are the first to understand that above all people is the reason for the growth of a business. Growth and development happen when unique talent is unearthed and is exposed to another unique talent.

Whether you are working for yourselves or aspiring to work for yourselves or just plainly looking to advance the career, you will accomplish much more in lesser time by having right people around you in your life. There is an old African saying that says, "When you wish to go quickly, go alone. But when you wish to go the distance, go together." Now there is an issue with this. Building relationships take up a lot of time, and it is not always productive as you are dealing with humans and not just deadlines. This will cost money and does not mean immediate ROI either. With the growth in our commitments and rise in the workload, it is tempting to stick with who we know.

However, like pretty much everything in life, in case your network is not growing for some reason, it is dying. Even when you are not in the market for new client relationships, fostering the current ones will be the priority each day. And as business mirrors the rest of the world in some ways, a more fruitful personal life is also just around the corner if you have committed to building relationships every day. What is the possible solution? Try to add relationship stacking to the list of daily habits. Think of it as an intentional and condensed session in which you spend time growing new and current relationships.

Starting Off

1. Start with committing to ten minutes every day for growing your network. Write it down on your calendar if you have to.
2. Prepare a list of all the skills or things of value which you can bring in a relationship. What skills are paid by people? Are you a leader, mentor, or a strong coach? Although this may be silly to apply to your personal life, it will be a good question to ask. What are you bringing to the table?
3. Take time out to jot down the names of people presently in your network. Categorize the network in groups. For example, friends, clients, colleagues, mentors, and family. You might also want to make notes on the people you are adding to the list. For instance, Frank (sports fan, marketing expert), Meg (loves arranging get-togethers, excellent host), and so on.
4. Identify three archetypes (example: business mentor) or people you may want to add to the network within the next six months. Where do find these people? What are the skills you have that will be beneficial for these goals?
5. Begin! Use the ten minutes every day to increase the relationships.

Here are three methods for getting you started on relationship stacking.

Option 1: Using Text Messages or E-Mails

Use the ten minutes every day to send messages or e-mails to the people from your list. Remember, do not just become a guy that checks in as, you are not their doctor. And also don't be the guy that sends cold e-mails asking them what their biggest problems are. Spend some time on Facebook or LinkedIn looking at what these people are doing these days. Ask queries that matter to them, and remember not to rush anything. People always know if you are being straight with them. You can send fifty text messages within a minute, but that doesn't mean you should go ahead and send them. Even a single one might be enough if it is sent to the right person. Another thing to remember is that not everyone will answer right away, meaning that you will have homework on your hands later on.

Option 2: Using Handwritten Cards

When did you write a letter to someone the last time? Although it might seem outdated, it means a lot to people to get handwritten cards in their mail. Find out who deserves thanks note from you in your personal or professional life. Can you make a colleague's day by showing to him that you actually care? Utilize the ten-minute relationship stacking time block to write a card to people that deserve it. The effectiveness of the option is something that has to be experienced. People love to get such cards, although it is just a simple gesture that can win you friends or fans for life.

Option 3: Long-Term Playing

Think about the long-term and high-impact activities you may wish to invest your time into. You could invest energy into it in the upcoming months. Use the ten minutes sometimes to find that out. Spend the first few minutes of the relationship stacking time to look over the agenda for the timing in the day where you may schedule activities with the persons in the network. Can you take some time off on Fridays once every two weeks to have lunch with one of the old clients? When was the last time you sat with your mentor and discussed something? Can you afford to take a day off and use it to go on a short weekend trip with your family?

The quality of life you're leading can be measured by the quality of your relationships, and one of the prerequisites for quality is consistency in efforts over a period, being able to play the long game. In case it is not already visible, let's leave you with a disclaimer—building relationships is not about being able to extort something from someone. The target of relationship stacking is to provide you with an easy vehicle to build relationships. It is a small chunk of time every day when you need to be honest and authentic with yourself and others. It is a way for you to be intentional in deciding who will be in your life at some given moment.

You will be getting nowhere in case you spent ten minutes daily trying to hard sell to strangers, being selfish, or lying. The initiative you took will be remembered the most, and the first impressions are important. People will remember you when you show them that you cared enough about them and their things to go for it first. This may be the most significant message of the chapter. It is your responsibility to grow your relationships. Do not let people in your personal or business life fall through cracks because they didn't reach out recently. There is all likelihood that they are sitting on the other side, thinking about the same excuses as you for the lack of time or resources. Remember there is always time available when you care enough. After all, nothing much is more important in life than spending time with people you care about.

Chapter 11: Habit Stacking to Improve Your Finances

Improving a financial position requires deliberate actions and discipline. Actually, when you think about it, the money you can keep depends basically on the choices you make every day. However, making intelligent financial decisions do not always require that you have to spend a lot of time. As a matter of fact, there are many small actions you can perform each day to improve your present situation financially.

1. Transferring funds: It is important to always be aware of how much money you possess and where it is kept. When you are aware of how much money you have, it can be decided better how to spend it or save it. Remember overdrafting and checks bouncing are bad and expensive habits that you need to avoid. Take a look at all bank and credit union accounts you have. Note the amount of money you have in these accounts. Make a decision about transferring the funds from one account to another or how to spend it on paying bills. It takes only five minutes.

2. Read personal finance articles: You could not be overeducated about finance. It is significant to be aware of how an economy works, and know your personal finance in order to make good financial decisions. Learning from others is always smart in order to save more money and avoid costly mistakes. Use search engines, such as Google, to find out articles about personal finance. It could be a daily piece or an advice column written by experts. It will definitely provide you with insights into personal finance and inspire you to make changes to your finances. This also takes just five minutes.

3. Collect loose change in a jar: A nickel here and a quarter there may not sound like much, but when you have collected all the change and kept it in one place, you can see how fast it adds up. Each time you add change to the jar you are basically adding to your savings, which are

130

growing over time. Check your purses, pockets, kitchen table, or other places you may leave the spare change. Collect all of it and place it in the change jar. Avoid the temptations to take out the change from the jar by keeping a lid on it. Store the jar inside a cupboard or a drawer. This takes about two minutes.

4. Write down the expenses incurred on the earlier day: Keeping track of your expenses is the smartest way of managing your personal finances. Write down everything you bought along with the figures of how much it cost. It will also give you an insight into your spending habits. Over time, you will notice different trends emerging out of your spending habits, and you will be able to decide where you need to make cuts in order to save money. Use notebooks or checkbooks to note down all the expenses from the earlier day. Keep the receipts so that this is made easy rather than trying to remember everything. By days, write down all the items and their prices, tax included. You may note whether you paid cash, credit card, or a check for the purchase. This will take up about three minutes.

5. Count the cash: When you are aware of how much cash you possess, you will be able to take correct decisions while spending it. It is significant to know how much money you have in case there is a bill that requires immediate payment. You also need to be aware of the exact cash you have when you shop in the stores that do not accept debit or credit cards. Not having sufficient cash for purchase will cause you to use credit cards that often lead to larger purchases than intended. You are also required to pay commissions on the purchases unless it is paid off immediately. Collect all cash from your purse and pockets for the day and count it. Place all this cash in your wallet and set some aside in case there is a need for specific expenses, such as for lunch and paying bills. It needs just two minutes.

6. Unsubscribe from junk catalogs and e-mails: Receiving junk e-mails and print catalogs offering discounts and promotions quite often leads to unnecessary expenditure. If you are saving 20 percent on a purchase, it is not a saving at all if you are spending $100 to save $20. By getting rid of these e-mails, you can take a break from the buying impulses and save money as a result. Go through your inbox and unsubscribe from the retail e-mail list. It is a statutory requirement to have an unsubscribe link at the bottom for all e-mails although it may take a few seconds to find it. All you need to do is click that button and then confirm. Also, look around the house for catalogs you do not wish to receive anymore. Call the company or send an e-mail and get your name removed from their mailing lists. You can use services such as UnRoll.me or Catalog Choice for streamlining the whole process. It takes just two minutes to get rid of the unwanted subscriptions.

7. Look for coupons for your necessities: There are many products that you need no matter how much they cost. So do not pay more than you need to for every item. By using coupons for essentials, like dish soap or napkins, you can save a lot of money. Go through the daily newspaper or browse on the internet for coupons that are required for necessary items, such as toilet paper, paper towels, or garbage bags. Cut out the coupons from the paper or print them from the net and put them in your wallet so that the next time you buy the essentials, you can use them. It takes about three minutes.

8. Pack your snack/meal and coffee: You can start making your lunch at home and bring it to work or make the coffee at home rather than buying it at the drive-through. Not only is this healthy for you but relatively cheap as well. Going out for coffee or lunch every day adds up fast, costing you many a dollar. It is easily possible to avoid the situation by preparing lunch and coffee at home at a fraction of the cost. Check your kitchen for the things you can use as a snack or as something for lunch. Place this item under your purse or with the car keys so that you will not forget to take them while going out. You can make the coffee at home and take it with you in a travel mug to the office. This requires about two minutes.

9. Find out things that are free to do: It is possible to go out of the home to enjoy yourself without having to spend any money. However, several people overlook this fact. Dinner and a movie afterward can cost a couple close to 100 bucks, which are your hard-earned money and could be spent on groceries or for paying off the credit card bills. By enjoying the free activities in your locality, you are allowing the extra income to stay in the house for more significant things that greatly benefit the personal finances. Check the local newspapers or websites for free activities listing you may enjoy. Find out the parks nearby, free concerts, movies, and community events. Select the ones you wish to do and write them down in your calendar so that you will not forget about the event. It takes three minutes to do this.

10. Set a limit for daily spending: It is significant that you have a daily spending limit when you are making an effort to improve your financial situation. The spending limits allow you to have extra cash and avoid too much spending on impulsive buying. In the morning, decide how much money you will need to spend today realistically. In case you have bills due for payments, take them into account. Choose an amount that does not allow impulse purchases or too much expenditure. This takes only a minute.

11. Plan the daily errands: Planning the errands for each day is similar to planning your budget for every day. This keeps you on track and in total control of the spending. Plan these errands in order to avoid places where you tend to overspend and visit the places where you need to go to in logical order. The planning will save time, money, and gas together. Note down the list of errands you have to complete. Then rewrite it again with the order in which you need to finish every task. Ensure that you stick to the list so that you do not go somewhere you didn't have to go and spend when there was no plan of spending. This takes about two minutes.

12. Turn off the lights and electronic appliances when not required: This happens to be the simplest way to save money. Turn off the lights and electronic appliances when not required in your office, home, or apartment. It can lead to a saving of a significant amount of money when it comes to the monthly light bills. It is significant to save money in this manner as it is easy, saves money, and helps the environment. Take a lap around the house, office, or apartment and turn off all the unnecessary lights and appliances. This requires just two minutes.

13. Do comparisons while shopping online: Making comparisons while shopping ensures that you are not overpaying for something you are buying. The bigger and more expensive the purchase, the more significant is the comparison shop. It helps you save money and make more educated buying decisions. Select an item you need to purchase. Look for the same item on at least three other retail sites. Check their features, availability, price, and other details to verify the best available deal. You need five minutes for this.

Chapter 12: Dealing with Habit-Stacking Disruptions

Habit routines normally start out reasonably well. You are excited about the new routine and eager to begin with the new changes. You will create a routine and see some immediate positive effects. But in real life, something always comes up and is in the way. The key is having a plan in place for when there are breaks in the habit-stacking routine for one reason or another. The reasons include sicknesses, vacations, and emergencies.

People quit the routines not just because of laziness but because some outside events derail their efforts for some time. These few days that go by without performing the routine quickly turn into a few weeks, and then what happens is that you don't know how to get restarted again. Luckily, there are some ways you can prevent this from happening and get back to the routines again.

Strategy 1: Have a Contingency If-Then Plan Ready

You must take for granted that some sort of disruptions will occur in the routines. It is just the plain fact. It is possible to accept these disruptions without being discouraged as they are pretty much expected. Always be prepared to condone yourself for the disruptions and being able to move on. You may be forced to stop the routine for a while, but rather than being down for not being able to follow through, turn the feelings into motivational thoughts for completing the routine come the following day.

One of the obvious examples of disruption is going on a holiday. This can easily obstruct your habit-stacking routine. This is because you are no longer in the place or working on the time frame of your everyday routine. When you have an if-then plan, it allows you to revive from the disruptions and continue the habit-stacking success story. The if-then plan is also called implementation intention and is based on finding the cues that cause you not to finish the routine. The idea here is to create a plan for the time when the cue takes place.

For instance, if one of your habits is checking your bank account balance each day online but on the day internet is not working. So do you have an if-then plan at hand? If you cannot check the bank account online, then you may go to the bank or call them and ask for the account balance.

Strategy 2: Know the Triggers

For creating an if-then plan, you must be aware of the triggers. Know your bad ones, which prove to be distractions and bad habits that make you slip up and have a negative impact on the habit- stacking routine. Keep track of the negative habits as this will help you in developing the routine. You possibly are looking to lead a healthier lifestyle but eat fast food habitually. Keep track of when this is happening and what is triggering it.

For example, do you skip lunch during the day and binge on the fast food? It is possible that you eat fast food only when you are sulking and are in a bad mood. These are the triggers that are significant to recognize so that you may develop an if-then plan to kick them off to the curb and keep on doing the positive changes. If you have packed snacks with you, then you will not be hungry on your way home and be tempted to visit a fast food joint.

The if-then plans are capable of doing battle with the bad habits, and they reinforce good habits. However, what if they cannot prevent you from quitting the habit-stacking routine totally? Take a look at the bigger picture. Are you missing one or two habits or skipping the whole routine? You must know how to get back into the swing of things in case it happens to you. Here is how.

Strategy 3: Reducing Overall Expectations

There is a fine line between the pressure that is on you while completing the daily routine and placing too much pressure on yourself. Additional pressure can lead to too much pressure, which causes a negative reaction, and that is exactly what you do not wish for. Rather than taking on too much and attempting to complete things that are more than realistic, concentrate on minimum but ensure that you are focusing on habits that are significant. While building your habit-stacking routine, always have this in your mind. It is easy to try to overcompensate when there is an emergency. It happens to everyone, but if you are filling your plate and it is too full, what is likely to happen is that the plate will tip over.

Strategy 4: Start Small Again

Starting all over again can be discouraging; however, it is mandatory when it comes to the habit-stacking routines. In case you need to start over, always start small. Concentrate on a few habits first in order to get back to the routine. The more you perform the small habits, the better your chances are of getting started again and completing the set. Be happy with small wins and focus on sticking to the routine rather than focusing on the routine length. Here you will have a firm grip on the routine, and you can add more to it. Do not forget to never miss a single day of the routine though.

Keep Going

Let's be practical. We all face those mad moments when we begin a good habit only to find the routine fizzling away a few days later. It is a natural part of a society that is overloaded and overstressed with info. You may find yourself starting and stopping a routine a few times. The actual secret to making a habit stick does not lie in individual habits. It is concentrating on turning the habit-stacking routine in an intrinsic routine. In case you find that you are not able to cope with the routine demands, then here is an example from Stephen Guise's mini habits. Think of the easiest and the stupidly small habit that will take minimal or no effort. Then concentrate on doing some of them every single day. Add tasks such as brushing your teeth, texting love messages, taking vitamins, or other such tasks like, say, reading an inspirational article every day.

The whole habit-stacking routine takes less than five minutes to complete. Therefore, you should have no issues following it each day. After it has become a daily ritual, you may add more challenging or complex changes to your lifestyle. And no matter what, keep going. The most significant takeaway from this book is to concentrate on routine and not the independent habits. This is true even while you are busy and overwhelmed by life. It does not matter if you have only completed a habit-stacking routine compromising of three actions that last a single minute each. The most important thing is to be consistent every single day.

Chapter 13: Selecting Triggers for Your Habit-Stacking Routine

The most vital part of any habit-stacking routine is getting started. This is the reason why it is significant to attach it to a cue or a trigger. The trigger is an action or an event that generates the beginning of your routine. It is similar to a green light at the start of a bike race. The habit triggers are commonly discussed negatively. More often than not, they are discussed in conjunction with bad habits, such as how the drinking habit brings on a smoking habit. But as the triggers can result in creating a negative habit loop, they may also generate good behavior, like waking up in the morning can be a trigger for brushing your teeth. After creating a habit-sticking routine, you need to select a trigger for the successful completion of the routine.

Similar to the building of the routine piece by piece, you should look at the characteristics of the triggers so that you can choose the one that will help you in taking an action. For example, while choosing a trigger, keep these things in mind.

1. An action or an event can be utilized as a trigger. For instance, rising up in the morning can be a trigger, or even eating lunch can be one.
2. This is simple. In case the trigger makes you work, you have less probability of doing it, and that means your habit-stacking routine will not work.
3. It needs to be automatic, like a timer going off at a certain time of the day.
4. New habits will not be good triggers. The trigger must be something you are doing presently every day.

After selecting the triggers, fix the following habit-stacking routine immediately after the event happens. The more you do this, the simpler and instantaneous it becomes. You can write yourself notes or reminders until the transition is being successful on its own. Do not worry if you struggle to make the trigger to habit contact at first. Quite often, it takes many people several weeks or even months before they automatically move the trigger to a habit.

Create a bond between the habit and a trigger, which will help you begin the habit-stacking routines every day. The key to success is repetition. Once the trigger is identified and followed every day, then it becomes a priority. The best way is to pick a time and location for the routine. For instance, if you pick your alarm clock as the trigger, it means that you need to set aside half an hour for completing a habit routine, which includes, walking the dog, taking vitamin pills, collecting dirty clothes, and placing them next to the washing machine. This is to be repeated every day, and you are doing it without even thinking about it.

Every time the alarm goes off, you must be ready to start the habit-stacking routine. Now similar to any new habit or activity, it takes some time to get used to the routine. You may miss a day or two, or you might be required to eliminate some other small habits. The key lies in sticking to it and ensure that you are doing it every single day. Remember not to start a routine before the alarm goes off and not even ten minutes after. In order to build the right connection, you must start the routine as soon as the alarm is ringing. Beginning too early or late causes a weak connection, and it will result in missed days and, as a result, less impressive results.

Conclusion

Now do not allow anything or anyone to stand in your way. Before starting, ensure that you are properly prepared for the task that lies ahead. Depending on your goals and habits, think about the time and things needed and ensure that they are in place beforehand. If you are concentrating on productivity, here are a few things to consider before starting:

- Go to bed early, meaning more time for the routine in the mornings.
- Buy and set up any necessary filing system.
- Find the right app or software to manage the time.
- Write down the important tasks in order of priority.
- Plan for a reward.

All of us have faced occasional obstacles or challenges. The trick is to note them ahead of time and then take the initiative toward overcoming them.

© Copyright 2019 - All rights reserved.